Give Us This Day
Year 1

GIVE US THIS DAY

Reflections for Each Day of the Liturgical Year

James McKarns

ALBA · HOUSE NEW · YORK

SOCIETY OF ST. PAUL, 2187 VICTORY BLVD., STATEN ISLAND, NY 10314

Library of Congress Cataloging-in-Publication Data

McKarns, James E.,
   Give us this day : homilies for each day of the liturgical year /
   James McKarns.
      p.   cm.
      Contents: v. 1. Year one — v. 2. Year two — v. 3. Saints and
   seasons..
   ISBN 0-8189-0611-1 (Year One)
   ISBN 0-8189-0612-X (Year Two)
   ISBN 0-8189-0613-8 (Saints and Seasons)
   ISBN 0-8189-0614-6 (Set)
      1. Church year sermons.   2. Sermons, American.   3. Catholic
   Church — Sermons.   I. Title.
      BX1756.M3398G58   1991
      251'.02 — dc20   91-7181
                                                                            CIP

Designed, printed and bound in the United States of
America by the Fathers and Brothers of the
Society of St. Paul, 2187 Victory Boulevard,
Staten Island, New York 10314, as part of their
communications apostolate.

Printing Information:

Current Printing - first digit   1   2   3   4   5   6   7   8   9   10   11   12

Year of Current Printing - first year shown

1991   1992   1993   1994   1995   1996   1997   1998

DEDICATION

These three volumes of homilies for
each day of the liturgical year are dedicated
to the memory of my father: Donald T. McKarns. He
frequently imparted to others didactic stories, wise
sayings and pensive thoughts. His school was the classroom
of nature and each passing season introduced a new teacher.
It was from him I learned many truths and lasting
lessons, which I have used as life-values.
Concerning the preachers of the Gospel, he
often said, "The good ones are those who
give you something to take home."

INTRODUCTION

My seminary professor of homiletics once made a statement which I have never forgotten: "Don't go to the pulpit," he said, "just to say something. Go with something to say." We certainly should always have something to say for our subject matter is lofty and dignified. Listeners are present and disposed to hear sacred ideas that will influence their lives.

Homilies should be rated as some of the most outstanding and inspiring talks in the world. Not only do we speak of the most challenging mysteries of life, but we also have such ideal conditions in which to convey our messages. There is an atmosphere of silence, reverence, pleasant surroundings, and respect. The list of advantages goes on like a litany. So if the homily falls short of this exalted image, and surveys say it often does, where is the Achilles' heel?

We always have to ask, "Did the homilist step into the pulpit with something to say?" I personally have a phobia about boring people, wasting their time by sounding empty. If I come to preach a homily which first has not excited me, how in God's name is it going to excite anyone else? I would prefer to preach without a shirt on my back, than to try to preach without a definite message in my heart. Never yet have I met a person who can stand in front of a congregation and successfully "wing it" without previous preparation.

If you, the reader, can find some inspirations in these pages which will excite and entice your heart to pour forth your own lofty wisdom, then you will have accomplished both your mission and mine.

As a directive for daily homilies let me leave you with a bit of advice from Dale Carnegie. "Find a good beginning and a good ending and put them pretty close together."

Year 1

MONDAY, FIRST WEEK OF THE YEAR
Heb 1:1-6 and Mk 1:14-20

We used to consider the letter to the Hebrews as written by St. Paul, making his fourteenth epistle. Modern Scripture scholars are convinced Paul did not write it and we don't know who did. In discussing the writer nowadays, we simply say, the author of Hebrews. The author shows in the very first chapter a fine knowledge of Jewish traditions, which are presented with a deep degree of scholarship. It is the author's conviction that God has spoken to the world through Jesus more clearly and intimately than God has ever spoken before. It is stated: "In times past, God spoke in fragmentary and varied ways . . . through the prophets" but now, "he has spoken to us through his Son." Divine revelation is no longer presented "in fragmentary" ways, but is consistent and well-designed, for it is presented by God's Son. Jesus has revealed the mysterious aspects of salvation, both by his words and life in a human body. The happy result is we have a much better idea of God. This better concept says God is kind and forgiving. God is close to us. Fear can give way to intimate love.

TUESDAY, FIRST WEEK OF THE YEAR
Heb 2:5-12 and Mk 1:21-28

There is a kind of innocent, human touch to this passage from Hebrews. It's refreshing to hear the author quote Scripture, while admitting he's not sure just where the passage is located: "Somewhere this is testified to. . . ." The passage says human beings are exalted. The thought is so captivating that the precise location of the text is secondary. It's not too important *where* it is said, but *that* it is said. We know the author was referring to Psalm 8; so the liturgy uses this psalm as the responsorial for today. This is a very uplifting psalm which proclaims the precious dignity of each and every man and woman. We, like the sacred author, may forget the precise chapter and verse of the text or the number of the psalm, but we should always remember the beautiful lessons being taught. God is ever mindful of us. We are made "with glory and honor." Human beings rate in the order of creation right next to the angels in heaven. This should make us love and respect each other always, for God loves each of us abundantly. We have all been elevated to a wonderful dignity.

WEDNESDAY, FIRST WEEK OF THE YEAR
Heb 2:14-18 and Mk 1:29-39

The evangelist, Mark, frequently pictures Jesus as being extremely busy. Some of his accounts of Our Lord's labors exhaust us, just to read them. In this passage, Jesus spent the day curing fevers, driving out demons, preaching, making comments and attending to many other activities, which were swirling about him. Following a night's sleep, numerous tasks were awaiting his attention the next day. Jesus rose early but avoided all contact with people and problems. Instead, he retreated to the desert and there was "absorbed in prayer." The word, absorb, means literally to suck up or take in, as a sponge collects water. If it were necessary for Jesus to give prime time to intense prayer, how much more compulsory for us? Have we ever been absorbed in prayer? Imagine being caught up in God's presence so completely that no noise would disturb our ears and gnawing tensions would not invade our hearts. Is there a busy day ahead for you? Spend some quality time absorbed in prayer and discover a rich source of strength.

THURSDAY, FIRST WEEK OF THE YEAR
Heb 3:7-14 and Mk 1:40-45

Today there is more desert-talk in the liturgy. The author of Hebrews, moved by the Holy Spirit, warns his readers to be in tune with God's voice. Do not rebel or harden your hearts, as the ancient Israelites did when they were being tested in the desert. That dry and barren desert area is in itself harsh and unattractive. Yet spiritually minded people are drawn there, not for what they can discover in the desert, but for what they can discover within themselves while they are in the desert. Jesus returns again to the desert after more ministering in the neighboring towns. What prompted him to continually return to that empty, arid wasteland? No doubt its voiceless days and still nights reminded him of the quiet peace of the world he left behind. I've heard of some retreat houses which contain a desert-room, where one can walk and sit on the sun-warmed sand and reflect. The world is very noisy with all the commerce of humanity and millions of blaring televisions. We should often, like Jesus, return to our quiet places to listen and hear the voice of God.

FRIDAY, FIRST WEEK OF THE YEAR
Heb 4:1-5, 11 and Mk 2:1-12

If God tells us our sins are forgiven we should consider the matter over and finished. When we continue to doubt and question the forgiveness, we are denying God's word. The critics of Jesus, in this Marcan passage, heard the words of absolution but saw no external results, thereby concluding nothing had happened. When his assertive voice produced observable consequences, making the paralyzed man stand up and walk, the crowd was struck with awe. True followers of Jesus should believe his words without having to see external results. Faith knows the deed is done, simply, by God's speaking, whether external results are in evidence or not. It is significant that Jesus told the healed man to take his mat with him. If he walked home without his mat, excitedly telling others along the way how he had been cured, they might not believe his word. His mat would serve as an observable piece of evidence that his words were true. Has God spoken some words which you find difficult to believe? "Why do you harbor these thoughts? Which is easier to say. . .?"

SATURDAY, FIRST WEEK OF THE YEAR
Heb 4:12-16 and Mk 2:13-17

Imagine Jesus being tempted in every way we are. We know what is happening within us better than any other person. How often we think there is no one in the whole world who has such bizarre and evil thoughts and temptations as we do. We are tempted to brag, exaggerating the truth to appear very important. We're enticed to lie when facing some difficulty or embarrassment. We, and our brothers and sisters, are tempted and, in fact, do steal, kill and live unfaithful to our vows and promises. We are tempted to despair, to be harsh to many and angry with others. There is even the temptation to deny our sins, telling ourselves they are not wrong. Maybe our denial is done in real honesty or perhaps out of fear of facing a demanding God. In the letter to the Hebrews, it says, Jesus "was tempted in every way that we are . . ." Therefore, we can turn to Jesus for understanding and merciful forgiveness for the sins we may have committed or thought of committing. What powerfully good news this inspired letter proclaims to the whole world and all the people who dwell therein! Jesus Christ, the Son of God, can "sympathize with our weakness."

Here are set forth the origin and purpose of the Hebrew priesthood, the foreshadowing of the priesthood in the Catholic Church. The priest is taken *from* the people and ordained *for* the people. The first step of Jesus toward acquiring his priestly office was to become a member of the human race. Following that he offered his most precious sacrifice for the people. The very nature of a priest is one who offers sacrifices and intercessory prayers to God. By nature Jesus was totally spiritual; human qualities were added later. We, by nature, are human and we strive to become spiritual. The Lord, by being both human and divine, became the perfect mediator between God and people. Jesus is also the victim; offered up by himself — of his own free will. The author says these heroic deeds of Jesus, took place "in the days when he was in the flesh." These are the days we are now in the flesh. We can join our sacrifices and intercessions this very day, with the sacrifices of Jesus. Daily we can live spiritually by offering our gifts, our time and especially our suffering to the Father, in union with Jesus the priest.

"Remember to keep holy the Sabbath," is a revered and ancient law. We would hardly think of disputing it. The religious leaders of the people in the Old Testament had defined the precise limitations which one should not transgress, in order to keep the Sabbath rest. Jesus breaks the law and allows his apostles to do the same. The reason: he had a different, a higher law to follow. For Jesus, human need superceded the written law.

Since the law came from God originally, Jesus tells the Pharisees they had not interpreted the law properly. They had been too literal and superficial. In making a reference to King David and his men, Jesus gives approval of what David did, even though he had technically broken the law by doing what was prohibited on the Sabbath. Jesus shows the older interpretation, at the time of David was the correct one. The Pharisees in later years had changed the interpretation. Thus Jesus upheld not the letter but the spirit — the original intent of the law. For Jesus, as for us, the real priority is not to be a slave to the law but to use the law, in the best way possible, to alleviate a human need.

WEDNESDAY, SECOND WEEK OF THE YEAR
Heb 7:1-3, 15-17 and Mk 3:1-6

To be shriveled is to be dried-up, drawn tightly or to have a lack of moisture. Our bodies are literally filled with fluids which keep us alive and well. The man with the shriveled hand was the symbol of a person who lacks the fluid needed to carry on a normal life. What a blessing he encounters to find Jesus coming to his rescue. The Lord gives him the water of life which wells up from within and releases his drawn up tensions so that he can function again. To "shrive" is an ancient word meaning to forgive in the sacrament of reconciliation. Jesus worked miracles of healing wherever he happened to be — even in the synagogue on the Sabbath. The Pharisees were law-conscious and not very people-centered. They could not truly appreciate the healing of the shriveled man. All they could see was that the Sabbath rest had been violated by Jesus and they concluded that he had no respect for either the law or the Sabbath. Jesus simply told them that peoples' needs are more basic than some laws. The Sabbath was made for people, not people for the Sabbath.

THURSDAY, SECOND WEEK OF THE YEAR
Heb 7:25 - 8:6 and Mk 3:7-12

We know how famous celebrities are protected by security guards when they move among the crowds. Many times there is a waiting car, near at hand, for the celebrity to make an escape from the melee which often accompanies their appearance. Jesus faced similar problems, as noted in this Marcan passage. The people in today's gospel try to reach out to touch, or shake hands with the Lord as groups of our times attempt to touch the famous of this world. He told his disciples to have a fishing boat ready for him so that he could put some distance between himself and the crowd. That same attraction continues to draw people to Jesus today. We come to our liturgies, private prayer, Scripture reading or meditation to be close to Jesus and receive a blessing. We come, especially with our afflictions, to receive a hoped-for cure. Beyond our personal needs, we should press close to Jesus to tell him we love him. Our pressures may push him into the boat, but our love will draw him closer to us.

FRIDAY, SECOND WEEK OF THE YEAR
Heb 8:6-13 and Mk 3:13-19

In this passage from Hebrews, the author reflects on how the Old Testament covenant with God depended on the Pharisees and Sadducees to enforce it. They were the "experts" who gave the official religious interpretations of the law for the people to follow. In the covenant of the New Testament, the people are expected to be more their own guides. Although the Church is present to offer guidance and direction, the basic decisions on how we will live our lives must come from within us. It is the natural law. This reading explains the natural law has been placed in our minds and written upon our hearts. It is very helpful for us, in our choice making, to solicit the opinions of other people, especially those who are deep-thinking and well informed individuals. Yet, ultimately, the choices and decisions rest with ourselves and our own conscience. Listen for a moment to what is happening inside of you. Are tensions destroying your inner peace or fears and doubts holding you back? Let God's natural law rule your heart and subdue these negative forces. You are a child of the New Covenant. The Lord has set you free.

SATURDAY, SECOND WEEK OF THE YEAR
Heb 9:2-3, 11-14 and Mk 3:20-21

When we plan to give a gift to a person that we love very much, we want to give something meaningful, unique and precious. We will search for the correct present or if we have a particular talent, we might personally make something. People spend numerous hours painting a picture, writing a poem, cross-stitching a lovely scene or making any number of beautiful creations for loved ones. In the Old Testament the unique gift offered to God was the blood of animals in sacrifice. The blood was seen as containing the very essence of life. God is the author of all life and, therefore, one of God's own precious gifts is returned as a present to the creator. Jesus offered a gift to his Heavenly Father in our behalf and he wanted it to be the most precious imaginable. The gift, therefore, was his own blood. He could not have presented a more priceless and intimate gift. Previously Jesus had said no one can manifest a greater love for another than to give one's life for that person. Jesus, therefore, shows the greatest love possible, with the giving of his own life-blood. Because of this unique gift for us, we can never doubt the love of God for his people.

MONDAY, THIRD WEEK OF THE YEAR
Heb 9:15, 24-28 and Mk 3:22-30

The "unforgivable sin" is mentioned in this passage of Mark. It is referred to as "a sin against the Holy Spirit." In essence this means that one would designate the highest good to be the most heinous evil — God is called the devil. A person can not be forgiven this kind of sin because the fundamental thinking of the individual is totally distorted. If forgiveness is to be a reality, then the sinner must first admit the sin and seek the Lord's mercy. In the case of the sin against the Holy Spirit, the basic conversion or about-face has not been made. The person has the world completely upside down. Yes is no, black is white, right is wrong and God is the devil. The section of Hebrews, read today, emphasizes the total goodness of God, showing Christ destroying sin with the magnanimous gift of his blood. The scribes, mentioned by Mark, are far from the thinking of the Hebrew passage. They say Jesus gets his energy and directives from the devil. They are guilty of a vicious sin of calumny. Forgiveness can only follow a change of heart and a seeking of the truth.

TUESDAY, THIRD WEEK OF THE YEAR
Heb 10:1-10 and Mk 3:31-35

People often have serious conflicts over how much time they should devote to their jobs and how much should be given to their families. The same situation was also present in the life of Jesus. While Jesus was at work this day, right in the midst of his talk before a large audience, his mother and some other family members try to call him from the dais to speak with him personally. Don't you wonder what in the world was so important that they would interrupt him at that time? We are never told what the urgency of the situation was. Jesus didn't comply with the request but gave a quip, similar to his temple-statement, when he was twelve years old. He states that those who hear and believe in him are as close to him as are his natural family members. Indirectly, the Lord was saying that his family bonds were based on faith rather than on blood lines. Therefore, he is already talking to his family. To the best of our knowledge he did not discontinue the lecture to speak with his mother and relatives as they had requested. It's exciting to realize that deep faith in God makes us as close to Jesus as his own natural mother and relatives.

WEDNESDAY, THIRD WEEK OF THE YEAR
Heb 10:11-18 and Mk 4:1-20

These words from the letter to the Hebrews are packed with rich images of the Lord's merciful love. God establishes a new covenant with his people. This new covenant was not our idea, but God's, manifesting divine goodness and care for all people. It tells us that we are now able to reflect within our own hearts and minds to discover God's directives for our lives. We won't have to search elsewhere. It's a return again to the theme of the natural law. I think one of the most powerful quotes in Scripture is found in this passage. "Their sins and transgressions I will remember no more." That would be an excellent quote to place above our reconciliation rooms, over our mirrors or any place where we could often reflect on its profound meaning. We need to remember that consoling statement when sickness or injuries befall us. Often on those occasions, we imagine this ill is present because of some sin we have committed. That type of punishment-thinking does God a disservice; making God appear as a revengeful person. In those and many similar cases, we are the ones who have not forgiven ourselves. We would be much better advised to spend more time praising God and less time blaming.

THURSDAY, THIRD WEEK OF THE YEAR
Heb 10:19-25 and Mk 4:21-25

We have a good chance of getting a smile from someone, if we first offer that person a smile. To get a letter, we often first need to send a letter. If we are expecting to receive a unique blessing, spiritual etiquette would say, we must first offer a prayer. How often we might complain about our situation and feel neglected both by God and others because we have not received something; but the first question to ask is how much have we given. Generosity is one of those talents and lights which are not to be hidden under a basket. Others need to see and know about our abilities and good works, for that causes them to consider how they can do better. Selfishness is difficult to overcome but examples of unselfish giving by others can be very inspiring to those who have become too self-centered. If we are generous with our time, money and mercy we can inspire and enlighten others. What we give, we get in return; that applies to both hurts and blessings.

FRIDAY, THIRD WEEK OF THE YEAR
Heb 10:32 39 and Mk 4:26-34

The author of Hebrews refers to the finding and accepting of Christ, as being "Enlightened." That enlightenment enabled the early Christian believers to endure suffering in a joyful manner, even as Jesus did. Do we see our faith in God as an enlightenment? There are so many mysterious questions pertaining to the whole spiritual world that we have no way of understanding them except by the light of faith. We can not logically reason to a satisfactory answer. The gospel emphasizes a common happening which we see everyday, but don't really understand. That is the growing of the seed. It is elementary to till the soil and plant the seed, but what would happen if we also had to make the seed sprout into new life? If the seed would refuse to grow, we couldn't open it as we would a car hood or TV set and twist or turn something to make it work. The seed operates on a different level — a mysterious, spiritual level. The spiritual world is much more mysterious than the physical and only deep faith in God can help us to understand it. Our faith provides us with wonderful enlightenment, enabling us to make some progress in knowing the "unknowable God."

SATURDAY, THIRD WEEK OF THE YEAR
Heb 11:1-2, 8-19 and Mk 4:35-41

Faith is very basic to our lives: not only religious faith but faith in general. In this section of Hebrews, there is a fine scriptural definition. "Faith is confident assurance concerning what we hope for, and conviction about things we do not see." I think that is a remarkable description of faith. It always involves something we don't see, but we have a conviction it does exist. The author wishes to present shining examples of faith as it existed in the lives of people in former times. The star witness is no surprise. We all knew it would be Abraham who would be marched across the sacred page. He is the one who obeyed and followed that challenging call from God at a time when people were not accustomed to God speaking to them. He was a most hopeful man and his hopes were vindicated. Sarah, his wife, follows right behind. She is remembered for her trust in God's promise that she would have a child in her old age. Each of us is somewhere in that long line of people who still have confident assurance of what we hope for, and solid convictions about the things we do not see.

The gospel speaks of a man in a truly terrible condition: existing in tombs, living among the dead. His strength, overpowering as it was, could not free either his body or soul from being chained within. It would be difficult to paint a more pathetic picture of a miserable person. An evil power had invaded, conquered and now controlled his every action. Presently, an even stronger force of goodness was moving toward him, in the person of Jesus. The sacrifice of 2000 swine was offered in order that one man would be set free and saved. Can we even begin to imagine what marvelous blessings the presence of Jesus can bring us. We are not as desperate as the man dwelling in the cemetery but we still need evil driven out, in order to be at peace. We also note in this reading from Hebrews how the saintly people in Old Testament times wandered about in deserts, in caves, in pain but in faith. To others they appeared to be freakish and foolish, but within they deeply honored God. Their lives were approved because of their faith. The author holds them in high esteem saying: The world was not worthy of them.

What kind of sickness, worry, depression or fears have been bothering you for a dozen years or more? Have you tried to find healing by consulting doctors, counsellors, or psychologists, but the problems just won't leave? If so, you can relate to this woman, with her twelve-year hemorrhage. Jesus is in our midst. We can come close to him and reach out to be blessed by his incarnate power. We can always draw near to the Lord, as this hurting woman in the gospel did. The presence of Jesus in the sacraments, especially in the Holy Eucharist, continually attracts believers to come and receive a healing grace. There are so many ways to touch the Lord. We do it not only in church or in private prayer, but when we reach out in loving service to others. Isn't it encouraging to know that even if Jesus is on the way to raise someone from the dead, it's not too much trouble for the Lord to stop and minister to hurting people along the way? Our abiding faith in Jesus enables us all to stand up and begin to walk again.

WEDNESDAY, FOURTH WEEK OF THE YEAR
Heb 12:4-7, 11-15 and Mk 6:1-6

The choice of words in this gospel gives us a clear insight into the nature of faith. The people did not believe in the deeper powers of Jesus. They took him only for face value. To them he was but another young man who had grown up in the vicinity. Because of their lack of faith, Mark says, Jesus could work no miracles there. Notice that it is not stated, he *would not* work any miracles but that he *could not*. Healing miracles generally require two things: something from the giver and something from the receiver. What must come from the recipient is a deep belief in the giver. If that is missing, the miracle probably will not take place. God may or may not work a miracle for us. But it is highly unlikely that there will be a miracle in our behalf if we lack full faith in the Lord. If we want a miracle in our life, remember we are part of the miracle-working team — God and us. The people in this passage were fascinated and amazed at the power of Jesus but didn't truly believe in him. There is a vast difference between being fascinated with the Lord and truly believing in him.

THURSDAY, FOURTH WEEK OF THE YEAR
Heb 12:18-19, 21-24 and Mk 6:7-13

Here the Hebrew people of the Old Testament are contrasted with the Hebrews of the New Testament. The passage shows a radical change of attitude in those who follow Jesus, from those who followed Moses. It was during their forty year desert trek that God spoke to Moses on Mt. Sinai. This mountain encounter visibly affected Moses, leaving him "terrified and trembling." He was afraid to look at God, face to face, lest he should die. Following his experience of meeting God, the people were afraid to look at Moses, face to face, lest they die. The thinking was not that God would maliciously punish them, but that the impact of the divine majesty upon them would be more than their human systems could endure. Quite opposite is the image of God as seen in Jesus, the one who appears to the people in the New Jerusalem. It is called here Mt. Zion, which is often used as a synonym for Jerusalem. Jesus has calmed the fears of the people and gently mingled with them, face to face. Free from fear we, too, can approach the Lord, sit at his feet and find peace.

FRIDAY, FOURTH WEEK OF THE YEAR
Heb 13:1-8 and Mk 6:14-29

The Rule of St. Benedict states that every person should be greeted and welcomed to the monastery or convent as though that individual were the very person of Christ. St. Benedict, very likely, got his inspiration for that directive from this Hebrews passage about hospitality. The inspired word says that this type of hospitality has lead some people to "entertain angels without knowing it." That was true in the case of Tobit, whose best friend was really an angel in disguise — Raphael. It's an overall call to show respect and not to take advantage of any person or group of people. We are to extend genuine courtesy even to those in jail. They may be looked upon as a lower class of society but they, too, have their dignity. Prison does not take away their right to basic respect. Regardless of the crime one has committed, a prisoner is still a human being. There is a goodness, a quality and a divine sacredness in all people. The church today calls us "The People of God." If we could see Jesus in one normally "unwelcome" person, there is no telling what beauty we might find within all individuals.

SATURDAY, FOURTH WEEK OF THE YEAR
Heb 13:15-17, 20-21 and Mk 6:30-34

Today we read the thirteenth and last chapter of the Book of Hebrews. This book has been providing us with daily thoughts for the last four weeks. The final chapter contains a brief summary of the entire letter and a concluding blessing. Note the key points of exhortation are: (1) Continue to offer a sacrifice of praise. This means not only are the priests to offer sacrifices on the altar but all people are to offer sacrifices of praise. Everyone is expected to proclaim God's goodness and love. (2) Do good deeds generously. These good deeds are sacrifices with which God is very pleased. (3) Obey the leaders of the people, that they may live in joy rather than in sorrow. An unhappy leader, religious or civil, makes life more difficult for the people. The blessing invokes the God of peace, who raised Jesus, the great Shepherd, from the dead. May God, in the blood of the eternal covenant, furnish you will all that is good, that you may do his will. To Christ be glory forever. Amen.

MONDAY, FIFTH WEEK OF THE YEAR
Gn 1:1-19 and Mk 6:53-56

In the creation story, from the Genesis account, there is no mention of God producing the wind or water. They are already in existence when the story begins. In the very first sentence they both are mentioned: ". . . a mighty wind swept over the waters." The wind is spirit, the breath of God. It is that vital element which is necessary for every second of life in all the creatures that breathe upon the earth. It is as ancient and necessary as God and also as invisible. It's everywhere, but we often say, there's nothing there. The water is also basic and nearly as old, in the Genesis account, as the wind. God shapes and forms it by the wind. Next to the wind, the water is necessary for life. We need it both internally and externally. Most of what we call our material self is composed of this primeval water. The creative God has given early notice of the essential nature of the wind and water. When we breathe the wind and drink the water, we are being transported far back into time, to our beginnings and beyond.

TUESDAY, FIFTH WEEK OF THE YEAR
Gn 1:20 - 2:4 and Mk 7:1-13

The original biblical story of creation is brought to its literary completion with the appearance of the first man and woman. The creation story began with the appearance of broad concepts of light, sky, land and the extraordinary variety of creatures in the world. Gradually it narrowed its scope on the sixth day to highlight the unique and precious aspect of all creation, which is that of human life. Following each day of creation, the statement is made that the work of that particular day is good. Notice that following the sixth day, when the first man and woman appear, the concluding statement is not only good but "very good." The teaching is

clearly presented that human life is exalted above all the other
kinds of created life. It's not just another step but a quantum leap.
We value and reverence all that is, for it came in some way from
the mind of God. However, we must especially honor our fellow
men and women, as well as ourselves, for the bible clearly
teaches we are the crown of all God's creation.

WEDNESDAY, FIFTH WEEK OF THE YEAR
Gn 2:5-9, 15-17 and Mk 7:14-23

Today we hear the second account of the creation. Once
again there is mentioned the beginning of all life and material
objects. This second account is older than the first and places a
particular emphasis on the origin of man and woman. In this
account, human life appears first and the reminder of creation
then follows. Thus the author shows creation in general is for
the use of humanity. The first account is a type of "naturalist"
version with its details of the world of nature. It gives the human
beginning little more than a passing nod. This second account is
the "humanistic" version, explaining how God makes man out of
the clay of the earth. If we were able to read this account in the
Hebrew language, we would appreciate the play on words here
between "Adam," which means man and "adama," meaning
ground. God plays the role of the potter who shapes living
objects from the clay. The Hebrews would say, God makes the
"adam from the adama." This primitive passage also tells of the
origin of the human soul, for here God personally blew his breath
into the nostrils of the man, causing him to become a living
human person.

Here the author (or editor) of this ancient Genesis account is explaining the origin of woman. There is a symbolic meaning to the term woman. The Hebrew word "ishsha" is woman, which is similar to "ishah," meaning her man or her husband. Just as these two words could easily blend together, so it is with the two sexes. Our terminology often reveals our theology about the equality of the two sexes. However, we must bear in mind that terms often have a variety of meanings. Perhaps some of the sexist terminology is not as demeaning as it may appear. Woman, here, is referred to as the partner or the helper of the man. That might be interpreted as being degrading but God is also often referred to as a helper to people. We are to be helpers and partners to each other. The helper is the stronger one. Therefore, the passage could be interpreted as meaning women are superior to men. In fact they are superior in numerous ways. But rather than debating who's more important, etc., the real beauty of the passage is seen in how each one complements the other. The two cling together in body and mind with no fear and no shame.

After all the efforts, in the first two chapters of Genesis, to show the uniqueness and exalted nature of the first man and woman, the author now presents them exhibiting a profound weakness. Evil, in the form of a serpent, challenges the best of God's earthly creation and this best and highest falls to the lowest level. The first man and first woman drag the rest of creation down with them. There is no clear description of the exact nature of the earth's first sin, but the sexual references to the fall are very obvious. It is said that the tree is in the middle of the garden; there is mentioned the touching; a sense of shame and a need to cover the middle of their bodies. The whole subject is treated, not in a literal, but in a parabolic manner. Beyond the sexual connotations, even more serious are the sins of pride and disobedience. In their garden of Eden Adam and Eve had been blessed with precious gifts and a delightful life. The name Eden has a close association with the idea of delight. God had such wonderful plans for all creation, but they didn't last long. These same tendencies and temptations still continue to pull us down. Just read today's newspaper and see how our original weaknesses remain with us still.

SATURDAY, FIFTH WEEK OF THE YEAR
Gn 3:9-24 and Mk 8:1-10

When we do something wrong, we often find it difficult to admit our mistake. When a person does frankly acknowledge a mistake or sin, we normally admire that individual, for everyone realizes how difficult it is to admit wrong doing. A young child, who even accidentally may have broken a window in the house, will often hide when he hears his father coming home. If there is a chance for children and adults alike to blame another for some sin or mistake, we often do that. These same traits are so clearly seen existing in our very first parents. Immediately after the fall, God calls Adam by his proper name for the first time. Notice the first question asked is: "Where are you?" We can see the terrible consequences of sin for it has changed both Adam and Eve. Adam is afraid and begins to hide from God. God gave him no reason to be afraid. The guilt is all within himself and he can't openly admit it. The first question asked of Eve is: "Why did you do such a thing?" She immediately says she was tricked and confused. Both had a difficult time with their first confession.

MONDAY, SIXTH WEEK OF THE YEAR
Gn 4:1-15, 25 and Mk 8:11-13

The Pharisees were the perennial negative critics of Jesus. They were the many little crosses he had to accept and carry every day prior to his big cross. Notice how they boldly stepped forward here and immediately started to argue with Jesus. They refused to take the Lord's words at face value. They claimed a sign from the heavens would enable them to place their faith in the Lord, but Jesus knew that even the most spectacular of signs would not convince them to accept him as the promised Messiah and certainly not as the Son of God, equal to the Father. The only sign they received from Jesus was that of a frustrated sigh, from the depths of his spirit. A sigh is the expression of a deep audible breath. It often implies a kind of hopelessness in a certain situation. Then the Lord simply boarded the boat and left. We can not answer every question to the satisfaction of every person. Some don't really want to know what we think, they just want to argue. We have all been in those situations where there's not much we can do except, like Jesus, give a sigh and say, "Good-bye, I've got to catch a boat."

TUESDAY, SIXTH WEEK OF THE YEAR
Gn 6:5-8; 7:1-5, 10 and Mk 8:14-21

In chapters one and two of Genesis, creation occurs and everything is pronounced good and proper. God is so pleased with all that has been made. Then, in chapter three, things begin to deteriorate. By the time we get to chapter six, the statement is made that all is going to be destroyed by the creator — it has all gone wrong. God was deeply displeased with the wickedness of man. It is stated: ". . . no desire that his heart conceived was ever anything but evil." God was looking for the same thing as the modern day Marines: "a few good men." He found one in Noah. Because of this one good person, the human race was spared as was the whole of creation. We should never think that a single individual is not important and able to literally improve the quality of life in general. One good person makes a difference — a big difference. I can't regulate how other people will think, nor control the ways they talk or act. I can, however, this very day make the world a better place by being one good person myself.

WEDNESDAY, SIXTH WEEK OF THE YEAR
Gn 8:6-13, 20-22 and Mk 8:22-26

After the purifying flood had scourged the world with its devastation, Noah sent out, from the ark, a peace-dove to determine if life was liveable again. The uninhabitable earth sent it back. In a very human touch, Noah reached out of the window of the ark, caught the dove in his hand and brought it back inside. After seven days, meaning another long wait, he made a second attempt. Again the earth returned the dove, but this time with a token of peace, in the form of an olive leaf. Things were improving and after another time of waiting, the dove was accepted. Now a newly purified life and love began to populate the world *again*. We, like Noah, can send out our wishes for peace, love and forgiveness. Often our proposals are rejected outright. We should not be discouraged. The second attempt may produce a hopeful sign and further attempts will then eventually cause peace and goodwill to begin to grow and blossom, where there was only hate and death. If enough people would begin to distribute peace offerings and well wishes to others, the world could learn to love again.

THURSDAY, SIXTH WEEK OF THE YEAR
Gn 9:1-13 and Mk 8:27-33

Some passages in the Hebrew Scriptures (O.T.) are to be rejected by the modern day Christian, for Jesus has given them a different meaning and a new spirit. The "eye for an eye" and "tooth for tooth" by today's Christian standards are considered barbaric. However we are aware that some national governments still follow this ancient law and numerous individuals, in their private lives, operate by these standards. The post-flood teachings on capital punishment, are highlighted in this passage: "If anyone sheds the blood of man, by man shall his blood be shed. . . ." We know how Jesus revised these ancient codes of conduct and restated them with a much different ending. Turning the other cheek, going the extra mile, loving our enemies and praying for our persecutors is easy to profess but extremely difficult to live each day. The U.S. Catholic bishops recently took a strong stand against capital punishment. The United States is the only country in the Western World that still has the legalized killing of killers. The Lord's teaching in this regard is very clear. Don't do it. Continually, we must acquire the mind of Jesus, if we are going to call ourselves Christian.

FRIDAY, SIXTH WEEK OF THE YEAR
Gn 11:1-9 and Mk 8:34 - 9:1

Someone said that the Church today needs to give more encouragement to people to carry their crosses instead of trying to help them find ways to avoid them. Hardship and suffering are not always negative and fruitless experiences. We might be exerting too much effort to make life easy and thereby losing the real appreciation for living. According to the Lord, we are not free to pursue every possible option we might wish. The good life as well as a full one will always include some heavy crosses and a disciplined path to walk. We do not save our lives simply by losing them, but by losing them for the sake of the Lord. That requires a strict discipline and this discipline is what makes a person a true disciple of Jesus. The two words: disciple and discipline come from the same basic root. A disciple is a disciplined person who is committed to following a leader. Whenever we carry an authentic cross, we will always be able to look ahead and see Christ leading the way, carrying his cross before us. What a tremendous security, knowing that, in his footsteps, we are moving in the right direction. Nothing worthwhile can ever be achieved without pain and discipline.

SATURDAY, SIXTH WEEK OF THE YEAR
Heb 11:1-7 and Mk 9:2-13

Imagine the radiant scene of Jesus in the state of transfiguration on picturesque Mt. Tabor. It can easily excite the imagina-
. on. One can see the delicate golden beauty of grace and good-
ress shining through his eyes, face and entire body. The unique
evc.t attracts both the newly recruited apostles and the leaders from the past — Moses and Elijah. Jesus is the sacred centerpiece of all the surroundings. His transfiguration, however, was not actually a miracle, for Jesus by nature was radiant within. Here the inner beauty was simply allowed to shine forth. The real miracle was that Jesus was not in a state of transfiguration continuously. He daily hid his real glory and appeared as just another ordinary person. This exposed inner glow could have drawn thousands of followers, but Jesus did not want disciples who were only fascinated with him. The Lord wanted people who would follow him because they believed in his words. He was not about to play the role of celebrity or miracle worker, simply to gather a following. We believe in the words of Jesus whether we

are on Tabor or standing at the ugly scene on Calvary. True disciples are followers and believers in all places for all times.

MONDAY, SEVENTH WEEK OF THE YEAR
Si 1:1-10 and Mk 9:14-29

Here is another wonderful incident, where the faith of one person (a father), elicits a miracle from Jesus for another (his son). It is on the strength of the father's faith and his words, that the young boy is freed from the possession of the evil spirit. We are not told where the father obtained his deep faith in Jesus but he believed not only in the Lord but also in the Lord's disciples. Notice he had first asked them to help the boy. Their faith in God's power to expel demons, was apparently too flimsy to accomplish the feat. The father had more faith in the disciples than they had in themselves. They could not expel the evil demon from this young boy, and Jesus publicly announces that it is because of their lack of faith. "What an unbelieving lot you are." There will soon come days in their lives when Jesus will not visibly appear on the scene and then the disciples will need to depend on the power of prayer and their own strong faith if their healing ministry is to continue. If we want to free ourselves of sin and evil, we can do it only by sincere faith in the power of God and in the power of prayer.

TUESDAY, SEVENTH WEEK OF THE YEAR
Si 2:1-11 and Mk 9:30-37

I think it would be an excellent idea to lift a sentence from this Scripture passage and paint it on the front doors of our schools: "Whoever welcomes a child . . . for my sake welcomes me" (Mk 9:37). If Jesus would have been telling children about his approaching death and resurrection instead of adults they would have listened intently and asked questions. The adults, however, his disciples, the same ones who had lacked sufficient faith to expel the demon, weren't listening to Jesus or caring about his ordeal. Their concerns were very self-centered. They wanted to know which one of them was the most important? Isn't it ironic how hard we will work, pay, fight, and even kill in order to be so called important. What really does it mean to be important, and why is it so desirable? Jesus says it doesn't amount to much. It's not something we will find somewhere in the future, but we find real importance by returning to what we used to be when we were little — childhood innocence. That's true importance! That's being most like God! If I can really trust God today as my loving Father, then I'll be really important in God's eyes.

WEDNESDAY, SEVENTH WEEK OF THE YEAR
Si 4:11-19 and Mk 9:38-40

There's a popular holy card on the market with this famous Scripture passage on it: "Anyone who is not against us is with us" (Mk 9:40). These profound words of Jesus encourage us to work with other churches and organizations in our common efforts. The world is full of people who are working for the improvement of life and a better society. Whether we are in medicine, law, education, science, religion or whatever, as long as we are promoting good and not evil, we are all working for and with each other and with the Lord. The passage has particular meaning for different Christian denominations. The original meaning of the passage when it was first spoken was that we are to see our brothers and sisters of whatever faith or denomination as doing good and accomplishing God's purpose when they don't actively oppose his will. The other may be a Buddhist, Hindu, or Jewish and we, as Christians, should see these people as being for us and with us, whenever they are not against us and strive to do constructive things for others. Loyal people with noble objectives form a strong united force for good. We are all working for common objectives even though we are proceeding from a different motivational stance and perhaps in different ways.

THURSDAY, SEVENTH WEEK OF THE YEAR
Si 5:1-8 and Mk 9:41-50

A conversion is a turning toward something. Sirach says we should not delay our conversion to the Lord. Isn't it amazing all the projects we postpone day after day? We have them on our lists of things to do but they easily get pushed aside. Conversion to the Lord doesn't mean that we are turning to God for the very first time. Even though we have long been believers, we still need to turn again to God each day in faith, trust, love and prayer. Since God is the source of goodness, truth and beauty, it is most natural for us to turn often in his direction. God is like a bright and beautiful light that easily attracts our attention. Instinctively we scan the eastern sky in the morning and the evening draws our attention westward to view the setting sun. Our conversion to God is to be much stronger than our aversion to the ugly and the evil. How tragic when someone becomes so confused that he has an aversion to what is good and a conversion to the evil. Since God is the fullness of reality, a turning to God is literally a facing of reality. Today we should try to turn our thoughts to him quite often and, in the turning, experience a conversion.

FRIDAY, SEVENTH WEEK OF THE YEAR
Si 6:5-17 and Mk 10:1-12

From the pen of Sirach, there comes today an enlightening passage on the subject of friends. The Hebrew author says we may have a thousand acquaintances but out of that large group only one would be our friend and confidant. We are reminded also that friends must be tested to prove that they are loyal. If you trust one whom you think is a true friend and that person breaks confidence in a delicate matter, you can be seriously hurt. We have captured many of the thoughts of Sirach's idea of a friend with the old adage: "A friend in need is a friend indeed." In today's Scripture passage, Sirach states that a faithful friend is three things: (1) a sturdy shelter, someone who will always be there in time of need to protect us; (2) beyond price, someone who is precious beyond material worth and who gives his or her all freely; and (3) a life-saving remedy, a vital person in our life, someone whose absence would impoverish our existence. Do we thank God each day and many times during the day for sending us our dear friends? How in the world would we ever cope without these loving and faithful people? We need to thank Jesus often also for his tremendous friendship. The Lord says he calls us, not his servants but his friends.

SATURDAY, SEVENTH WEEK OF THE YEAR
Si 17:1-5 and Mk 10:13-16

Again Jesus turns to one of his favorite subjects — children. Here, as in the incident of the boy possessed by a demon, the disciples demonstrate their lack of real understanding of Jesus. One would think that they, who had accompanied the Lord on so many of his journeys and had heard him address various crowds and seen his reactions to so many situations, would have known his unique love of children. Had they been observant, they would have known his mind and would not have prohibited the children from coming to him. We might conclude that the disciples were not as observant as they should have been. So here Jesus gives another public rebuke to his followers. This reading from the gospel of Mark, much like the one this past Tuesday, extols the virtues of children and uses them as the real models of Christian virtue. We might find much to assist us in our living the Christian life by reflecting on our own childhood days. In our growing up have we lost some of our candor and simplicity only to become stilted and artificial in our relationships with others? Whatever happened to our first innocence? Perhaps a good Christian definition of an adult would be: "One who has grown up to become a mature and responsible child."

MONDAY, EIGHTH WEEK OF THE YEAR
Si 17:19-27 and Mk 10:17-27

The individual who is sincerely trying to reform his or her life is given a lot of hope in this first reading from the book of Sirach. To such a person Sirach says, God "provides a way back; he encourages those who are losing hope." This is a very encouraging thought to ponder especially during the Lenten season of the year. The person who is living a good life is not really "home free." There is always the challenge to do better. The challenge is presented in this passage of the gospel according to St. Mark. The good man in the gospel is enthusiastic about the possibility of serving Jesus, so he runs up to meet him. Although he has been faithfully living all the commandments, he is told by the Lord to be less attached to his material possessions. If he could forsake his loving attachment to his earthly treasures, then he truly would be approaching Christian perfection. He found that discouragingly difficult. And so, at times, do we. And still we must try. Both the sinner and the saint have an obligation to persevere in order to find salvation. No one, apart perhaps from our Blessed Mother, achieves complete perfection in this life. No matter what level we now occupy, there is always a higher one to strive for, a constant struggle to become better.

32 GIVE US THIS DAY

TUESDAY, EIGHTH WEEK OF THE YEAR
Si 35:1-12 and Mk 10:28-31

It's a common gospel theme that the more attractive the possessions we give up in this world, the more we will be repaid in the world to come. That's the teaching which Jesus conveys to Peter, following Peter's somewhat self-serving inquiry about the reward for abandoning all in order to follow the Lord. Jesus assures Peter and the others that they will be blessed a hundredfold with all the things which they previously did not have, or at least have in such abundance. Jesus says they will be most graciously blessed, not only in this life, but also "in the age to come." Just how we are to receive a hundred brothers, sisters, mothers and children is not clear, though it obviously refers to the fact that in following Jesus we become members of an enormous family whose ties are not restricted to blood bonds. The statement is somewhat poetic and it also means that if we give up anything in order to acquire the Lord, God's presence within will be worth a hundred times more than any or all the other possessions we might otherwise have had. We note here, too, that Jesus identifies himself with the gospel. We encounter the Lord in Sacred Scripture as surely as we do in the sacraments and in one another. So if we preach some highly charged Scripture text and it causes controversy, resulting in our suffering, then we are suffering persecution for Jesus and we will receive our reward.

WEDNESDAY, EIGHTH WEEK OF THE YEAR
Si 36:1, 5-6, 10-17 and Mk 10:32-45

James and John, in this incident, play the role of the "spoilers." They spoiled what should have been a deeply spiritual and sympathetic conversation between Jesus and his disciples. The Lord had just taken the Twelve aside and immediately began to discuss with them, clearly and confidentially, the dreadful events which awaited him in Jerusalem. There was no parabolic talk here. All was open and understandable. Jesus tells them what will happen to him in the Holy City: the chief priests and scribes will condemn him; he'll be mocked and spit upon and beaten; they will kill him but, in three days, he will rise again from the dead. This is as open and clear as it can get. What a marvelous opportunity for an in-depth dialogue with Jesus about all of these things, for it is obvious here that he really wanted to talk. The dialogue never took place, though, for Zebedee's two sons most brashly shifted the conversation away from Jesus and his coming passion to themselves and their hopes for high positions in the future. We do that, too, whenever we fill the air with our petitions instead of listening intently to the Lord in prayer. Somehow we must learn to forget our personal desires when we pray and let our hearts be enlightened by a deeper attentiveness to God's divine will in our regard.

THURSDAY, EIGHTH WEEK OF THE YEAR
Si 42:15-25 and Mk 10:46-52

The Book of Sirach, formerly called Ecclesiasticus, or the Church Book, here speaks of the mighty truths about God which are frequently proclaimed in church. The thoughts are both lofty and profound. We read that God's knowledge is all embracing. It encompasses everything. All past happenings and the entire future, yet to be unfolded, is in the mind of God. Every phase and part of creation has value for it can be traced to God. The glory of the Lord fills the world. After telling of the wonderful qualities and works of God, the author breaks into a prayerful praise of this mighty and loving Lord of the universe. In such an immense world of magnificent creations, as the gigantic sun, moon and planets, we by comparison might feel very insignificant. Here Sirach comes to our support with the teaching that no part of creation is made in vain. Sirach says these are not just concepts he has heard about, but they are the works of God that he has seen. From these expansive and lofty teachings about the nature of God, the Church Book continues to instruct us, give us dignity and makes us appreciate our wonderful creator.

FRIDAY, EIGHTH WEEK OF THE YEAR
Si 44:1, 9-13 and Mk 11:11-26

Mark relates certain incidents at this time in the life of Jesus which give a strong indication that the Lord was perhaps more than a bit annoyed. The normally patient Jesus becomes infuriated with both people and trees. It's a curious statement made early in the gospel, that Jesus went into the Jerusalem Temple in the late afternoon and "inspected everything there. . . ." You get the impression that he was investigating the quality of their worship. Perhaps someone had made a complaint to Jesus about buying and selling in the temple area. Apparently the inspection proved nothing wrong. The next day, however, returning from a night in Bethany, Jesus saw and cursed a fig tree because it had no fruit. But Mark adds, "It was not the time for figs." Then he returned to inspect the temple again. Had the people buying and selling in the temple known of the fig tree incident, they might have cleared out. Jesus came to the temple with the same zealous aggression he levelled against the tree. He upset tables, drove some merchants out, terrorized the others and called them all a bunch of thieves. We, like Jesus, will have highs and lows. Spirited adrenalin is a part of us. It could lead to sinful destruction, or as in the case of Jesus, to needed reforms for the good of all.

I like the statement made by Sirach where he says: "I will give my teacher grateful praise." He calls wisdom his teacher, but that wisdom had to be conveyed to him through other teachers. We have all had many human teachers who have given us much wisdom. We have national days set aside to give honor and thanks to various groups of people; such as mothers and fathers, grandparents, nurses, secretaries, bosses, etc. It's so fitting, therefore, that we also have a day in May designated as "Teachers' Day." The gifts good teachers offer their students are lifetime treasures. Have we ever sent a note of thanks? Imagine the thrill for a person to receive such an unexpected letter of appreciation, especially after many years. These are the dear and patient people who so unselfishly assisted us to acquire wisdom. It is understandable that Sirach would offer such exalted praise to his teachers for he also was a teacher. No doubt he, too, would have been delighted to receive notes of thanks from his former students. We are expected to be thankful and offer praise and gratitude to those who have so helped us to acquire the basics of life. God's wisdom has taught us many concepts and one is to express our gratitude to the people who have truly blessed us.

One of the corporal works of mercy, as taught by the Church, is to bury the dead. Tobit had dedicated himself to that task long before the Church made such a pronouncement. Today is the first of six readings from this curious book of the Hebrew Scriptures. It is judged to be wisdom literature rather than historical. Tobit is a displaced person in a foreign land. Living there with his family, he has not forgotten to observe his childhood teaching from Israel. In his thinking and conduct there is a simple piety. If he is faithful to his religious background, God will provide for and protect him, his family and the other Hebrew exiles. His virtues are evident, not only in his respect for the dead and his devotion to bury them, but also in his desire to share his Pentecostal meal with some hungry stranger. A powerful lesson from the theology and good works of Tobit is "regardless of how difficult life may be, you can always discover those with bigger problems." When we respond, as Tobit did, to the needs and service of the less fortunate, our problems are always diminished or even disappear.

TUESDAY, NINTH WEEK OF THE YEAR
Tb 2:9-14 and Mk 12:13-17

The Pharisees and Herodians were sent to trap Jesus in his speech. They began by paying him a genuine compliment. "It is evident," they said, "that you do not act out of human respect but teach God's way of life sincerely." You wonder if they were secret admirers of the Lord. Very likely they were impressed by the genuine sincerity of Jesus and inwardly ashamed of their own lack of genuineness. They must have been uneasy with their double standards — praising Jesus while at the same time trying to trip him in his speech. Even though they were less than sincere, Jesus gave a demonstrative answer to their question. As on many other occasions, the Lord asked his inquirers to give a portion of the answer. When they acknowledged the head and inscription of Caesar, Jesus made his point. Sometimes we might be more impressed with the powerful people in this world than we are with the Lord. When we act thus we are not rendering to God what is God's. We could never pay a tax to cover the cost of the death and resurrection of Jesus. Therefore Jesus chooses to be our savior and king, free of charge. We render respect and support to both Caesar and Christ, but our deepest and most heartfelt loyalty is obviously to Christ Jesus.

WEDNESDAY, NINTH WEEK OF THE YEAR
Tb 32:1-11, 16 and Mk 12:18-27

The new bride and groom were very compatible. It was noticeable to all. Someone remarked: "That wedding was made in heaven." All agreed. In this passage, Mark quotes Jesus as saying: "There are no weddings in heaven." Even the vows pronounced say: ". . . until death do us part." When death comes, the marriage ends. A person may continue to think of their deceased spouse as still their husband or wife, but that is no longer the case. Here Jesus gives another simple but powerful answer to the Sadducees, who like the previous Pharisees, were attempting to trap Jesus in his speech. Their plan was to refute his teaching on the resurrection by appealing to this obviously hypothetical marriage case. Jesus is the best teacher on eternal life we could ever expect to have. How difficult for him to convince others of his doctrines. We often think we're so knowledgeable about many subjects, including realities in the spiritual world and in the life beyond. Yet we, in practically all cases, know painfully little. We are always students, the Lord alone is the teacher.

THURSDAY, NINTH WEEK OF THE YEAR
Tb 6:11; 7:1, 9-14; 8:4-7 and Mk 12:28-34

Here is portrayed a typical example of an ancient Near East marriage. The entire agreement is made between the young man and the bride's father. The bride is not even informed that she is about to be married. We speculate if Sarah would have fallen deeply in love with Tobiah and didn't want to lose him, would she ever have informed him of her seven previous marriages and her very frightening track record. It would be very scary for anyone to think of marrying a woman who had been married seven times previously and all seven husbands had died on their wedding night. Since Sarah is not making the arrangement, the question is mute, but her father explicitly makes it clear to Tobiah. Tobiah is unafraid of Sarah for his friend Azariah, who is really the archangel Raphael in disguise, has told him how to protect himself. It's encouraging to realize that even though a situation may appear very forboding because of the past, divine assistance can provide renewed hope. Situations can become exactly the opposite from what they previously were. If we live in the continual presence of God, we can conquer all fears and find happy success.

FRIDAY, NINTH WEEK OF THE YEAR
Tb 11:5-15 and Mk 12:35-37

The thought of Tobit and Anna — sitting at home for a long time awaiting the return of their son, Tobiah — reminds one the elderly Simeon and Anna coming to the temple each day, awaiting the arrival of Jesus. The day Joseph and Mary entered the temple carrying the child in their arms, the old people recognized the Lord and hugged him tenderly. Simeon then expressed his contentedness. He was ready to die, since now his earthly life had been fulfilled. He had seen the Christ Child, his salvation. Both Anna and Tobit in our first reading expressed their willingness, too, to die; once they had seen their child home safely. The fish which Tobiah is carrying is regarded as having amazing healing powers. The cataracts are here symbols of a kind of blindness or separation from God. The power of the fish (Jesus) loosens them so that they can then be easily removed. The New Testament symbol of Jesus is the fish. Healing of souls, sight to the eyes, movement to paralyzed limbs would become the trademarks of his ministry. Tobiah here is an Old Testament type of Jesus — the healing savior.

SATURDAY, NINTH WEEK OF THE YEAR
Tb 12:1, 5-15, 20 and Mk 12:38-44

Jesus was a public figure. There can be no doubt about that. He frequently mingled with the crowds and was often the center of attention because of his cures and other miracles. The Lord was usually the person up front, giving the lecture, rather than the one sitting with the others listening. Although so much in the public eye himself, in this gospel he passes judgment on the scribes for the way they act in public. What did Jesus do that made him so different from the scribes? Basically, Jesus says, he was in the crowd to be of service; the scribes were there to be seen. That is the accusation in this gospel. They liked to wear their flowing, very expensive robes, wanted seats of honor at banquets and respectful greetings in the street. They tried to impress people, even poor widows, to get their money. They feigned their prayers in order to appear holy, not to please or appease God. All this disgusted Jesus and he publicly told the people not to fall for their deception. How and why do we mingle with people? Is it just to be seen? To put in an appearance? In every crowd, couldn't we be of service by giving encouragement to some, sympathy to others and genuine caring love to all? That's the way Jesus worked the crowd.

MONDAY, TENTH WEEK OF THE YEAR
2 Cor 1:1-7 and Mt 5:1-12

Paul refers to God as "the Father of mercies and the God of all consolation." The concept is that not only are we individually sinful but, as a collective race of human beings, we have a long history of offending God. In spite of our poor spiritual record, God has bestowed divine forbearance on us and still refrains from punishing. God continues to show mercy even when justice demands that we should be punished. All those concepts are inherent in the meaning of mercy. The consolation comes when we have suffered with Christ in some physical, emotional or spiritual manner. Following the suffering — which we will endure because of Christ and because we are with Christ — we will find that, in our suffering, the Lord was with us through it all. The point is that mercy is a gift freely given from above, simply out of the goodness of God. Consolation is somewhat different from mercy. To find consolation we must invest some of ourselves into a suffering effort for the sake of Christ. Christ will enable us to be victorious and so we will find consolation. How fortunate for us, to be cared for and loved by the Father of mercies and the God of all consolation.

TUESDAY, TENTH WEEK OF THE YEAR
2 Cor 1:18-22 and Mt 5:13-16

Paul assures the people of Corinth that he is consistent in what he says and does. Some of his detractors were claiming that he made big plans but didn't carry them to completion. Paul declares that he keeps his word with the same consistency with which God does. We all know those people who state one thing one minute and something opposite the next. What they think and say at any particular time depends on the person with whom they last talked. Jesus, St. Paul tells us, was always a "yes-man," but only to his Father. When Jesus faced the pain of drinking the bitter cup in the agony in the garden, he said "yes." When he was about to die on Calvary, he said "yes." The Lord never refused to do the will of his Father. When we pray to the Father, Jesus taught us to speak to God as he did: "Thy will be done." Each time we say, "Amen," we are saying "yes" to God. We often utter that conclusion to our prayer so thoughtlessly that we forget that it is a deep and binding commitment. Could we not say our "Amens" with greater conviction today?

WEDNESDAY, TENTH WEEK OF THE YEAR
2 Cor 3:4-11 and Mt 5:17-19

In this passage there is one especially noticeable statement: "The written law kills, but the Spirit gives life." Here Paul is contrasting the Old Law and the New. In Judaism, from which he had recently departed, almost every move was regulated by the written law. Their commandments were numerous, but people were expected to know and observe each of them. Regardless of one's disposition or even understanding of the law, there was an obligation to observe it entirely. Perhaps one did not agree with a certain law. That was no excuse for neglecting to observe it. The law was to be carried out, not according to the way an individual would see it, but according to the interpretation of the religious lawyers, Pharisees, etc. More to the point, even understanding the written law still didn't give a person the strength to follow it. Therefore the law was the occasion of one's "dying" spiritually. The New Law, symbolized by the "Spirit," gives life because the Spirit allows one freedom of choice, instructs one in truth and, most important of all, gives the person who is trying to be faithful the necessary grace to do so.

THURSDAY, TENTH WEEK OF THE YEAR
2 Cor 3:15 - 4:1, 3-6 and Mt 5:20-26

In the Old and New Testaments, there are many references to women wearing veils. This would be expected since veils were part of their normal garb. Moses wore a veil for a different reason. It covered the radiance of his face after he had spoken to God. The veil hid his face so the people wouldn't be frightened and also so that they would hear the voice of the God speaking through him and not be distracted by the brightness of his countenance. Paul uses the veil to make the point that those who do not understand the gospel of Jesus have their minds covered with a veil. The truth of the gospel shines out so brilliantly that it would be impossible not to recognize it unless people deliberately covered their eyes to avoid seeing it. Certain happenings and trends today may make us think that the world is deliberately veiling its mind to the truths of God's holy gospel. Yet there are numerous signs of hope and goodness, too. If we can not see these positive and encouraging people and projects, then we, too, are like those who have covered their minds with a veil. Look about today. Make contact with someone face to face. Try to sense in them the presence of the invisible God. The world is full of his loveliness.

FRIDAY, TENTH WEEK OF THE YEAR
2 Cor 4:7-15 and Mt 5:27-32

Paul makes it clear to the Corinthians that living the Christian life is no picnic. There will be continual fears, hardships and doubts, but the good news is: "There's always a way out." These negative forces can make life difficult but they can never defeat us. Jesus has seen to that. It is ultimately God's grace which will sustain us. Notice the litany of difficulties which we can expect and the corresponding responses of divine grace. We are afflicted, but not crushed; we have many doubts, but there is no need to despair. We are persecuted, but in those times God does not leave us. We will be struck down, but not destroyed. Jesus had to die first, and then be raised to life again. In our journey through this world we are often like Jesus on his way to death. We must follow in his footsteps. At those times it is essential to remember there is a tomorrow for us, as there was in the case of Jesus. There is a resurrection in our future. In summary, Paul is preaching the paschal mystery of the death and resurrection of the Lord. That's the basic meaning of living our life in Christ: we must die with him if we are to arise with him in glory.

SATURDAY, TENTH WEEK OF THE YEAR
2 Cor 5:14-21 and Mt 5:33-37

A new creation has taken place in the world, according to Paul; it's the death and resurrection of Jesus. The Lord is like another Adam, who ushers in an updated and spiritually improved order of earthly life. According to Paul's thinking, if we believe in Christ and his mighty deeds, namely, his death and resurrection, we have already undergone death ourselves, "since one died for all, all died." We are accustomed to thinking of Jesus as having died for us, but this passage emphasizes that we actually died *with* Christ. Imagine, we have died and risen to new life in union with Jesus. Our faith, in other words, makes us a new creation. We are spiritually existing now as if the fall of Adam had never occurred, for Christ has undone the damage of the original sin in the garden of paradise. Look at the marvelous qualities we possess and the outstanding deeds we can accomplish in Jesus, since in him we have become a new creation. Our salvation has already been accomplished and all believers have a share in the promise of that new and eternal life. We celebrate this wonderful accomplishment of our salvation in the sacrament of baptism.

MONDAY, ELEVENTH WEEK OF THE YEAR
2 Cor 6:1-10 and Mt 5:38-42

When someone strikes you on the face, blackens your eyes or bloodies your nose, it's only natural to fight back in similar fashion. Many would think that would be the proper response, but Jesus has a different idea. The Lord says to accept the hurts and insults which come your way without resistance or future revenge. That's the daily test we face in many ways, whether in thought or word or action. The first type of reaction is natural; the second is deeply spiritual and supernatural. Jesus chose the second type of response, where one returns love for hate. The martyrs and saints in general are honored because they followed his teaching on this point of moral conduct. We, too, occasionally follow the second way but more often it seems our reactions to personal hurts and insults are more natural than supernatural. The Christian law of non-retaliation is difficult to follow, and some believe it is absolute foolishness and very impractical even to try. They say if you live that way, people will constantly take advantage of you. And that's probably true. It is difficult, but it's what the Lord did and taught and, for that reason alone, it remains not only a lofty ideal but one that we ought to practice.

TUESDAY, ELEVENTH WEEK OF THE YEAR
2 Cor 8:1-9 and Mt 5:43-48

There is a wonderful secret contained in the gospel reading for today. The secret is revealed in answer to the question: "How can I eliminate my enemies? This is the answer: "Make them

your newest friends." The passage contrasts the law of the Old
and New Covenants. Jesus grew up hearing how he should love
his fellow citizens but hate his enemies. When he started preaching, he reversed that old teaching. "Love your enemies and pray
for your persecutors," was his message. It was not very popular
and still isn't. The Lord continually challenged his own people and
all who heard him to break out of the their narrow patterns of
thinking and to expand their views into broader considerations.
This new Christian code of morality has a wide range of consequences affecting everything, from our national security to our
personal possessions. A truly Christian nation would forgive past
attacks made upon it by another hostile power. The victim
country would even pray for the well-being of the nation that had
attacked it. Local enemies and persecutors would be forgiven.
The opposite reaction would be one of hatred and revenge. If
everyone would cooperate, it would work. Enemies would be
destroyed by becoming friends.

WEDNESDAY, ELEVENTH WEEK OF THE YEAR
2 Cor 9:6-11 and Mt 6:1-6, 16-18

This section of Matthew's gospel is recognizable as being
the gospel for Ash Wednesday. We might think it is applicable
only to Lent — like an actor who always plays the role of hero or
villain and thereby becomes role-typed. The advice was meant
for all people and for their daily living situations — it's not just
seasonal. Therefore, everyday is a good time to give alms to the
poor, not just during a penitential time. Everyday we are expected to offer prayers and devotions to God. Perhaps we could
make the stations of the cross at various times of the year.
Likewise, fasting should not be limited only to the Lenten season.
Fasting, along with prayer, was recommended by Jesus in order

to have the power over the evil spirits in this world. Make for yourself a spiritual program that you will follow throughout the year. Give high priority to works of charity, sincere prayers, devotions and fasting. This is the recommendation of Jesus, which he preached in the Sermon on the Mount, at the beginning of his public ministry. More important, the Lord used these as guidelines for his own daily living.

THURSDAY, ELEVENTH WEEK OF THE YEAR
2 Cor 11:1-11 and Mt 6:7-15

In the days before Vatican Council II, we often began and ended many of our meetings and classes with the Our Father. Recently we feel a need to be more original. When someone opens a meeting with the Our Father these days, others may think that person isn't very innovative and that traditional prayer isn't as fitting as a spontaneous one. That, of course, is foolish thinking, for how can you improve on the prayer taught by Jesus himself in response to the appeal of the Apostles: "Lord teach us to pray"? If we do use the Our Father, I think it should be said slowly and in a very meditative manner. Jesus himself places into this prayer our common needs. "Our Father" — imagine God's wanting to be known and called our Father. The phrase "in heaven" is such a lofty concept that we can linger over it for a very long time. Where is heaven and what is it? Then there's the request for necessary food for body and spirit and the plea to be spared from harm. There are so many deep and wonderful ideas which this prayer addresses within us. We should allow ourselves at least five minutes to say this prayer privately, and publicly we should never rush through it.

FRIDAY, ELEVENTH WEEK OF THE YEAR
2 Cor 11:18, 21-30 and Mt 6:19-23

If Paul would not have bragged to the Corinthians about his sufferings and disappointments in the course of serving Jesus, we would never have known of his many hardships. Instead of trying to determine or remember what he suffered, it is more fruitful to discover why he endured these many trials. The reason, why, can be traced directly to his love of Jesus. The public whippings, sleepless nights, floods, etc., were all accepted as testimony and witness that he loved the Lord. By serving the Lord in such an elegant manner, Paul was acquiring spiritual treasures, which taxes would not take and inflation would not erode. How do we feel about the pains and difficulties which we must endure to serve the Lord and to offer genuine love to each other? If we are like this energetic apostle, who gave his entire life to the service of the gospel, we, too, will discover that the price of any pain or difficulty is very small, in comparison with the treasure we hope to acquire.

SATURDAY, ELEVENTH WEEK OF THE YEAR
2 Cor 12:1-10 and Mt 6:24-34

Here we have another of those cases where Paul says he doesn't want to boast but he does, not to promote his own glory but for a higher reason. He writes in the third person to somewhat diffuse his bragging, but it is evident that he has experienced close encounters with God. Paul clearly remembers when this mystical vision occurred — fourteen years ago, perhaps around the year 45 based on the composition of the letter. It is not to be confused with his vision on the road to Damascus, where he experienced his conversion-vision. This passage is literally filled with intriguing concepts of mysticism, grace, weakness, spiritual strength and the power of Christ. A key sentence stands out following his mention of the "thorn in the flesh." It is the Lord's response to him, and it could be God's words to any of us who feel we are too weak to fight life's spiritual battles: "My grace is enough for you, for in weakness power reaches perfection." Perhaps like this fiery apostle we, too, should learn to be content with our many weaknesses and persecutions, for if we allow ourselves to be powerless for the sake of Christ, then we are truly strong.

MONDAY, TWELFTH WEEK OF THE YEAR
Gn 12:1-9 and Mt 7:1-5

This passage from Genesis sings the praises of Abraham, who at this point was still called Abram, and sets him before us as a courageous pilgrim of faith. Here Abraham, at age 75, launches out with his wife Sarai, Lot, his nephew and a small number of servants. They are on their way to the Land of Canaan to build an exciting future for themselves and to found a new nation. At age 75 his work is just beginning. This world-renowned patriarch has become the model and inspiration for people of all ages but especially the elderly. One is easily reminded of a modern day man of whom Abraham was a type — Pope John XXIII (formerly the patriarch of Venice). He launched out on his major mission in life at the age of 76. Like Abraham, Pope John had a change of name with his new calling and in many ways broke from former traditions to revise many past practices and re-energize the Catholic Church. All of us can catch the excitement of Abraham if we are willing to trust and walk in faith. "Abraham people" rejoice not so much in the "week-ends," as in the "week-beginnings," with all the marvelous opportunities which lie ahead.

TUESDAY, TWELFTH WEEK OF THE YEAR
Gn 13:2, 5-18 and Mt 7:6, 12-14

There was a famous Jewish rabbi, who taught in Jerusalem about 30 years before Jesus was born. He continued teaching several years after Our Lord's birth. His name was Rabbi Hillel. Tradition says that one day a student asked Rabbi Hillel if he could explain the whole law while he, the student, stood on one foot. As the student held one foot in his hand, Rabbi Hillel replied: "That which displeases you, do not do to another." He smiled at the student and added: "This is the whole law; the rest is commentary." Hillel was the grandfather of Rabbi Gamaliel, St. Paul's teacher. Our Lord, himself a rabbi and most knowledgeable of the law and the outstanding teachers, would certainly have read Rabbi Hillel. In the gospel today, Jesus summarizes the law in the same fashion as Hillel, although Jesus puts it into a positive framework: "Treat others as you would have them treat you." This well known verse in Matthew (7:12) is now known to us as the "Golden Rule." It still applies and is the basic model for many of our decisions. Whether it is stated negatively, as by Hillel, or positively, as Jesus put it, is not that important. It's not how we say it, but how we live it that counts.

WEDNESDAY, TWELFTH WEEK OF THE YEAR
Gn 15:1-12, 17-18 and Mt 7:15-20

When God told Abraham he would have a child of his own, Abraham believed although he was 100 years old. Abraham accepted the promise without the need for any more confirmation. Then God told Abraham he would be able to take possession of the Land of Canaan. This, though, he found too difficult to believe without a sign. The inference is that it is easier for a 100 year old man to father a child than to acquire ownership of a portion of real estate in the Holy Land. The same scenario still continues in that area of the world today. No one is willing to give up any land for the sake of peace or love of neighbor. The sign requested by Abraham was fulfilled and the ownership was conferred by God in a covenant with Abraham. We take many promises of God on pure faith without any specific signs, other than the basic sign of God's love for us. This is especially evident in the death and resurrection of Jesus. That is a sign for all times and places that salvation history is steadily moving to its fulfillment. What began with the promises to Abraham will be fulfilled in the future eschaton. Jesus promised it and he will do it.

THURSDAY, TWELFTH WEEK OF THE YEAR
Gn 16:1-12, 15-16 and Mt 7:21-29

Although Abraham's desire for an offspring was very strong, the text would imply that Sarah had an even stronger need for a child — any child — even one by her servant. The servant's child could legally be claimed by the person who "owned" the servant and raised as her's, rather than that of the natural mother. When a wife was childless, it was presumed she was at fault rather than her husband. The wife, therefore, was under a type of reproach as long as she had no child. Sarah's desire for a child was more important to her than her exclusive marital rights to her husband. It is ironic that she is the one who suggests her husband have intercourse with the servant girl. Again the marital exclusiveness is secondary to the possession of a baby. Many of the ancient Hebrew concepts are radically different from our Christian ones. This passage should make all parents very thankful for their children and see them as real blessings and gifts of God. Children not only enable human life to continue into the next generation but they, in a very real way, give purpose and meaning to the present generation as well.

In this passage we find the bible's first mention of the practice of circumcision (Gn 17:10). God tells Abraham explicitly that "Every male among you shall be circumcised." The reason circumcision was chosen to become the sign of the covenant is not absolutely clear. The Hebrews circumcised the baby boys eight day after birth, but some other cultures circumcised at the time of puberty, or in preparation for marriage. Its origin may have been hygienic or a symbol of approaching manhood, but here it acquires a religious dimension as a sign of the covenant. From this point on in Scripture, the term, "circumcised," will signify being clean and belonging to the covenanted people. The term, "uncircumcised," will signify unclean, ungodly and someone or something to be avoided. It is often used symbolically as in the expressions "uncircumcised ears," or "heart," etc. Although Jesus was circumcised on the eighth day after birth, as was Paul and others, the Church teaches this is in no way required to be a Christian. Our external Christian rituals have value only if the mind and heart are in tune with God's eternal covenant with us.

This gospel passage is an impressive testimony of the faith of a man who was not a Jew or a Christian but an officer in the Roman Army. The centurion, as his title indicates, was in charge of 100 soldiers. This particular centurion, who sought the assistance of Jesus to heal his suffering son, exhibits a profound belief in the spoken word. He dealt with the power of the word each day. Signals, commands and orders were essential for a well-functioning army. The centurion may delay in giving the word to his soldiers about some project, but once the word was spoken, then he knew the command would be carried out. In our military today, the same importance is attached to the orders given. Failure of a subject to obey the commander could result in a court martial. This man sees Jesus possessing impressive power over people in a spiritual and healing way. Thus, there is no need for the Lord to be present, just give a command, as the centurion does and wonderful results will happen. Can we have such deep faith in the powerful words of Jesus, that we feel sure those spoken words will be fulfilled?

MONDAY, THIRTEENTH WEEK OF THE YEAR
Gn 18:16-33 and Mt 8:18-22

The Lord had promised Abraham that the city of Sodom would not be destroyed if at least ten innocent people could be found living there. It happened that the city was soon destroyed so, apparently, ten innocent people could not be found. The only innocent ones in the town, it appears, were Lot, his wife and their two daughters. Those who were spared can thank Abraham for here playing the part of the intercessor — bargaining both for his brother's family and for the people in general. The Lord does not become angry with Abraham, for he was only trying to save as many people as possible. After all, that was his mission. The first section of this reading states how Abraham was singled out by God to direct his posterity in the way of the Lord. Perhaps we don't emphasize enough, as we used to, the intercessory mission of the Blessed Virgin Mary and the saints. It is a mission in which we all share. Abraham, our Old Testament "saint," here demonstrates for us an excellent model of intercession. We can bargain with the Lord, just as Abraham did. Jesus understands; remember He is Jewish too.

TUESDAY, THIRTEENTH WEEK OF THE YEAR
Gn 19:15-29 and Mt 8:23-27

For the Israelites, the sea was something to be feared. In it were all kinds of monsters which could not be detected until they would attack a person. God's power and fury was thought to be stored in the deep. Jesus understood the power of the sea, but did not worry about all those real or imaginary dangers present within it. He could comfortably go to sleep in the boat. If the boat should sink, he could simply walk to the shore. The same waves that lulled him to sleep frightened the apostles. Although fishermen, their fear of this raging water was quickly expressed. It was an understandable fear, for fishermen often lost their lives on that treacherous sea when it was in a rampage. Both the sea and their fears were calmed by the voice of Jesus. The apostles had forgotten to place their trust in Jesus who, although he was silent, was still in the same boat as they. God often seems asleep and silent in our lives, especially when we find ourselves facing danger and fear. How important for us to remember what the apostles momentarily forgot, namely that Jesus is always near, indeed he is within us. Our faith and love of the Lord should be enough to carry us through any and all tough times until we are brought to a safe and peaceful shore.

WEDNESDAY, THIRTEENTH WEEK OF THE YEAR
Gn 21:5, 8-20 and Mt 8:28-34

Isaac was finally born after his parents, Abraham and Sarah, had waited for nearly 100 years. Now with her own baby, Sarah no longer felt inferior to her maid, who had given birth to another of Abraham's sons. Sarah now forbade the half brothers to play together. She reasoned that Ishmael, Hagar's son, was not good enough for Isaac. She likewise made the decision, against her husband's wishes, that Ishmael's mother was not good enough to work in the home any longer either. Hagar, who had served them long and well, suddenly found herself dispossessed of home and job and sent off into the wilderness. In her suffering and abandonment, she hears the sound of God's voice. He has come to her assistance. Often, it is in the wilderness that God meets and speaks to those who trust in him. Ishmael now has blessed promises placed upon him in prayer. Isaac becomes the human link between Abraham and the Israelites as Ishmael is the human link between Abraham and the Arabs. These two warring groups of Middle Eastern people continue, today, their long standing divisions which began the day when Sarah ordered Hagar and Ishmael to leave the house.

THURSDAY, THIRTEENTH WEEK OF THE YEAR
Gn 22:1-19 and Mt 9:1-8

Abraham is known as the man of many virtues. Especially characterized by profound faith, we read in today's account another momentous event in his life, which added to his already established image. He is asked to offer up, in sacrifice to God, his own son, Isaac. His older son, Ishmael, has already been lost to the wilderness, having been sent there along with his mother, Hagar. Now Abraham is asked to permanently part with his beloved younger son, Isaac, too. Although filled with pain at the request, he understands this deed to be the will of God and, therefore, must be accomplished at all costs. One can only imagine the fierce reaction of his wife Sarah to this venture. Nonetheless, Abraham is determined to do the bidding of his God. Isaac becomes the type of Jesus who later would be asked in sacrifice. Like Jesus, he carries the wood for his offering up the hill. We know that Isaac was spared, at the last minute. Jesus was not. But he was reinstated in the resurrection. God, in this passage, is not mean or morbid, but he is testing the faith of Abraham. We hurt so badly when asked to give up little things. Abraham was requested to offer up his most precious gift, and still he was ready to do it. A religious commitment can be painful.

FRIDAY, THIRTEENTH WEEK OF THE YEAR
Gn 23:1-4, 19; 24:1-8, 62-67 and Mt 9:9-13

Jesus uses the call of Matthew as the occasion to teach a lesson about sickness and health. A person who has sinned needs the healing touch of Jesus, just as any sick person needs the ministry of a physician. When we are physically ill, we are not ashamed to tell people about our condition. In fact, many could, and do go on for hours about their illnesses; how they began and the manner in which the person is affected. These same people, who will reveal a half dozen illnesses and the symptoms of each will often deny they have any spiritual illnesses at all. The common phrase is: "I don't do anything wrong." We don't have to have a heart attack or a stroke in order to be sick. We don't need to murder someone in order to be guilty of sin. When someone asks, "How are you?" we think only of replying about our physical condition. Our response is: "I have a cold, a sore toe, a bad headache," etc. Imagine a spiritual reply to the question, "How are you?" "I'm not too good today because yesterday I told a lie, lost my temper, was very proud," etc. We need Jesus to heal us, whether we want to admit it or not.

SATURDAY, THIRTEENTH WEEK OF THE YEAR
Gn 27:1-5, 15-29 and Mt 9:14-17

This story from the 27th chapter of Genesis is one of the best known and most often discussed in all of the Old Testament.

It would make a good plot for a modern-day soap opera with its strong role models and well-defined characters, its exposition of greed, favoritism, jealousy, deception and bitter resentment. It has puzzled many of the wisest minds of history, including that of St. Augustine who wanted to uphold the dignity of Sacred Scripture but also to be logical. His conclusion was: *Non est mendacium, sed mysterium* — "It's not a lie but a mystery." Today, I think, we would simply have to say: "It was a lie and all of the above mentioned deficiencies are present." Rebekah is the instigator of the whole plot, but if we were to make inquiry about her motives, she probably would explain why she did it and why she felt justified in doing so. No doubt, she felt that the future of the family would rest better with the mild-mannered and peace-loving Jacob than with the rather wild and carefree Esau. Was it the blessing which enabled Jacob to be such an achiever and an outstanding personage of the Old Testament? Would he have done just as well without his father's blessing? We never will know for sure. That, too, is part of the mystery.

MONDAY, FOURTEENTH WEEK OF THE YEAR
Gn 28:10-22 and Mt 9:18-26

This gospel touches two subjects we fear most — sickness and death. The suffering woman had been laboring under her serious health problem for twelve years. That's another way of saying "a very long time." Touching the tassel of the Lord's cloak was her way of reaching out to Jesus in faith. We certainly don't think any kind of mysterious medicine or rays came from Jesus to cure her. She was healed from within herself. The Lord identified the real source of her healing. He said: "Your faith has made you whole." Jesus was the occasion for the healing within herself to be released. The source of the cure was internal, and Jesus caused it to function. The sequel was even more impressive. This was not a restoration from sickness to health but a restoration from death to life. The family of the little girl was thinking about her funeral, but Jesus thought of nothing less than restoring her to the fullness of life. Can we have so much trust in Jesus that a faith-healing could happen within us today? Our need may be spiritual, emotional or physical. The problem may have existed for a long time or be of short duration. We are not dead as long as Jesus is nearby. The Lord will take us by the hand and raise us up to life again.

TUESDAY, FOURTEENTH WEEK OF THE YEAR
Gn 32:23-33 and Mt 9:32-38

It must have been very difficult for anyone to associate with the Pharisees. They were convinced of the correctness of their views on every question. What they didn't know, they imagined. So, often they are presented as being narrow minded and unbending and those who told "the truth," exactly the way it wasn't. The incident in this gospel shows the Pharisees at their worst. Jesus had worked the wonderful and liberating miracle of expelling a demon from a man who was mute. The Pharisees could not rejoice that this man was finally freed. They wouldn't even inquire of Jesus how the miracle had been accomplished. Rather, they framed their own prejudiced thoughts into words and accused Jesus of performing this miracle with the help of the devil. There is no way they could have sincerely come to this conclusion. It had to have stemmed from prejudice and hate. A Pharisee was one who could not be joyfully mystified, or say: "Wow! That was terrific!" We need to be careful that we don't feel, like they, that we must have all the answers. Real faith always keeps us guessing, for the blessed Lord Jesus continually surprises.

WEDNESDAY, FOURTEENTH WEEK OF THE YEAR
Gn 41:55-57; 42:5-7, 17-24 and Mt 10:1-7

The story of Joseph is one of the Bible's most beautiful, especially in the areas of mercy and forgiveness. Joseph is sold as a slave to a slave trader. Although he had begged for mercy from his brothers, he received none. Many years later, there comes a day, when Joseph is in a position, to make them beg him for mercy. He is able to be harsh with his brothers for only three days, then they are released from their confinement. Joseph had a very sensitive heart, for at the end of their confrontation, he had to turn aside and weep in private. The story should inspire us to be forgiving of others who have hurt us. Even if our best friend, or brothers and sisters have rejected us, we still need to offer them our pardon. Let us recall the forgiving love of Joseph when we reach out for the handshake of peace. This gesture is meant to say, "We are on good terms, not only with those beside us, but with everyone." That is the disposition which should be in our hearts. It's a "Joseph gesture" — a sacred reaching out to neighbor before we reach out to receive the Lord in Holy Communion.

THURSDAY, FOURTEENTH WEEK OF THE YEAR
Gn 44:18-21, 23-29; 45:1-5 and Mt 10:7-15

This section of chapter 44 from Genesis is power-packed with intense emotion. It is difficult to read it without tears blurring your vision. Scripture scholar, Fr. Eugene Maly, calls Judah's speech, "one of the outstanding pieces of literature of the ancient world." It was given about 1700 B.C. Judah is interceding on behalf of his brother Benjamin, for he had assured their father that Benjamin would be returned unharmed. Little did Judah know that, as much as he loved Benjamin, Joseph's love for Benjamin was even greater. Joseph's intense, hidden emotion could no longer be sustained. What dramatic words: "I am Joseph." His first question was about his father's health. Again, to convince them, he had to repeat: "I am your brother Joseph, whom you once sold into Egypt." We see his sense of total forgiveness when he easily dismisses his misfortunes as "God's will." Jesus knew the story of Joseph and imitated his forgiveness. The Lord taught us the same lessons as Joseph. We are called to be one family, who serve one God, with one mind, one heart and one will.

FRIDAY, FOURTEENTH WEEK OF THE YEAR
Gn 46:1-7, 28-30 and Mt 10:16-23

There is an old expression which is sometimes uttered when one is surprised: "Land of Goshen!" The real land of Goshen is mentioned in this passage from the 46th chapter of Genesis. This Egyptian territory is located north of the Delta region. It is the choicest of grazing land, where the Pharaoh's own cattle were pastured. It was there that Joseph was reunited with his father after many years of separation. Joseph's sensitivity must have been at fever pitch as he awaited the arrival of his father. The text says he harnessed his own horses the morning his father was to arrive, and personally hitched them to the chariot. Perhaps he was up so early there was no one available to assist him. Soon father and son were reunited after many years and they embraced for a long time. What a wonderful and fulfilling surprise in the Land of Goshen. Our abiding hope encourages us to expect many joyful blessings and surprises, if we continue to pursue honesty and truth, as did both Jacob and his son, Joseph. Land of Goshen! People really do love, care and forgive each other. Life can be exciting.

SATURDAY, FOURTEENTH WEEK OF THE YEAR
Gn 49:29-33; 50:15-24 and Mt 10:24-33

The strong sense of family tradition shows forth in these passages. Jacob has definite plans regarding where he wishes to be laid to rest. He very explicitly stated that he wanted to be buried in the field of Ephron back in Canaan. It was only there he felt he could rest, for that was the plot of ground together with the "cave that was therein and all the trees" that his grandfather Abraham had purchased precisely for a family burial ground. There, too, he would be at rest in the presence of those with whom he had shared his life. Buried there were both his grandparents, Abraham and Sarah; his parents, Isaac and Rebekah; and one of his wives, Leah. These outstanding and world-famous people were finally laid to rest together in that one small piece of ground known as Machpelah or "The Field of Ephron" in what is today the West Bank city of Hebron. Fittingly the first book of the Bible closes with the death of Joseph. He has proven himself to be genuine and consistently forgiving. There is no revenge within his heart. He is a man far ahead of his times. Over a thousand years before Jesus told the world to turn the other cheek, Joseph had already done it. Will you be remembered as a person who turned the other cheek, before you closed your eyes and turned to dust?

MONDAY, FIFTEENTH WEEK OF THE YEAR
Ex 1:8-14, 22 and Mt 10:34 - 11:1

Today, liturgically, we begin reading from Exodus, where the initial sentence clarifies the reason for what is about to follow. It explains why the Israelites were persecuted and is the key to understand much of the continuing trouble in that area of the world today. The statement is: "A new king, who knew nothing of Joseph, came to power in Egypt." We can just imagine the bitter complaints which were uttered against the Israelites. They would be viewed as foreign intruders and accused of taking the Egyptians' jobs and occupying some of their country's best land. The complaining Egyptians did not appreciate the gigantic contributions which Joseph and his fellow countrymen had made to their nation. In the U.S. today we find those who may have some negative thoughts about Spanish-speaking people, forgetting that Christopher Columbus was financed by Spain. What do we remember of King Ferdinand and Isabella today? A sense of history in our hearts gives us a better understanding of current situations. We owe so much to other countries, such as France for example, for our beginnings, but we too quickly forget. Every minority in this country has contributed to our present well-being in ways which will never be fully appreciated. We can not be isolationists for, without the help of others, we would not be what we are.

TUESDAY, FIFTEENTH WEEK OF THE YEAR
Ex 2:1-15 and Mt 11:20-24

We have just listened to an account of the birth and early life of Moses. He is one of those famous people whose name is a household word. Moses became Israel's most important lawgiver, freedom fighter and friend of God. Whenever we think of him, we envision a very saintly person. Thus we have the expression: "Holy Moses." God watched over this three-month-old baby, floating in his little papyrus basket in the river. He was providentially blessed with a royal education and inwardly inspired for his future mission. As a young man, Moses killed an Egyptian, who had abused a fellow Hebrew. When the Pharaoh tried to capture and punish him, Moses fled the country. "Holy Moses," wasn't always such, but he grew to both physical and spiritual maturity. God's love and mercy are also given to us. We, like Moses, should not dwell on past sins and failures, or lowly origins, but look ahead to our mission in life. Each of us is called to be a freedom fighter and friend of God.

WEDNESDAY, FIFTEENTH WEEK OF THE YEAR
Ex 3:1-6, 9-12 and Mt 11:25-27

God reveals to Moses something of his own intimate nature — that of fire. It is alive and glowing in a burning bush, yet does not consume the bush. This phenomenon calls attention to the presence of God, for it is the nature of God to give warmth, light and to purify that with which he comes into contact. All is done in such a gentle manner that the entity is not destroyed. Moses is told to remove his sandals so his feet may be in direct contact with the ground, which is made sacred by the presence of God. It is also impressed upon Moses that he is to return to this same sacred mountain of Horeb (a. k. a. Sinai), to receive from God the "Ten Commandments." It is a favorite practice of God to call people to the tops of mountains for sacred communications. Jesus, himself, often made his way to a mountain top for prayer and spiritual retreat. Many saints have found the mountains equally attractive. Perhaps we should all have a mountain retreat — our own personal Mt. Sinai. Any intimate prayer experience is like a trip to the mountains, since it puts us in touch with God.

THURSDAY, FIFTEENTH WEEK OF THE YEAR
EX 3:11-20 and Mt 11:28-30

The conversation at the burning bush gave Moses a precious glimpse into God's nature. Now he is entrusted with the possession of God's own personal name. God's name had not previously been revealed to any other person. The divinely beautiful poetic name disclosed to Moses was: "I Am Who Am." The name speaks of a strong and everlasting existence and an origin that had no beginning. It would be quite proper to address God by his poetic name. We could say: "Let us now pray" to "I Am Who Am." Our names, as God's, are very personal. We value both our Christian or given name and especially our last name, or surname, as very precious. Surnames often reveal our various nationalities, but our first names also speak of our origins and have unique meanings. Alexander means defender; it is of British origin. Robert is bright and William is resolute; both are from the ancient German or Teutonic language. Barbara is foreign, from the German. Jonathan means God has given, from the Hebrew. Andrew is the strong one and Agnes is pure; both from Greek. "I Am Who Am" means existence, always present. The Hebrews translated it as Yahweh.

FRIDAY, FIFTEENTH WEEK OF THE YEAR
Ex 11:10-12, 14 and Mt 12:1-8

Every springtime the Jewish people celebrate the sacred feast of Passover. It commemorates their liberation from slavery in Egypt and the beginning of the long trek to their homeland. Today's first reading from Exodus gives the original story. Jesus celebrated Passover and used the occasion of the event for the setting of the Last Supper — complete with the eating of lamb. Jesus, likewise, offered himself on the cross as the victim lamb. The lamb is closely attached in time and temperament with the passover theology. Jesus, through his sacrificial death, gave freedom from sin to his past, present and future followers. The paschal mysteries are at the very core of our faith as Catholic Christians. Each day, to some degree, we relive the death and resurrection of Jesus. This Mass and each one celebrated, calls to mind again this life-giving event. We need not see ourselves as prisoners of time, age, duty, and fear because Jesus has liberated us through the paschal mysteries. The Lord has led us out of slavery as Moses led his people out of Egypt. Set free from the burden of sin and moving toward the Promised Land, we have had a new and better passover.

SATURDAY, FIFTEENTH WEEK OF THE YEAR
Ex 12:37-42 and Mt 12:14-21

The circumstances of this passage are noteworthy. Dreaded plagues have been visited upon Egypt because of Pharaoh's decision to retain the Israelites as captives. Remember, it was the Egyptian people who had originally requested them to leave and Pharaoh had granted them permission. The Pharaoh of the Exodus was Rameses II, who came to power in 1290 B.C. This marked Israel's time of departure. The text says the Israelites were in Egypt for 430 years, meaning that they had come to Egypt in the year 1720 B.C. It appears they wanted to leave as peacefully as possible. The text states that Moses led them from the capital city of Rameses to Succoth. That is the coast route to Canaan. The more direct route would have been straight across the Sinai Peninsula but that may have invited military confrontation with the Egyptian army. Moses literally went out of his way to avoid conflict. The Exodus is an intriguing story of God's people returning home. The most dramatic events are yet to unfold as they approach a showdown at the Red Sea. In the most severe trials, God walks with his people.

MONDAY, SIXTEENTH WEEK OF THE YEAR
Ex 14:5-18 and Mt 12:38-42

Some people place much trust in particular religious signs. For example they close their eyes, open the Bible and point to a verse. They then use that verse to direct their lives since they believe God lead them to it. One young lady was trying to decide whether to get married in June or August. She said if the phone would ring within the next five minutes she would choose June. The phone didn't ring. Neither did the wedding bells — in June or in August. The scribes and Pharisees, in this gospel, wanted to see a sign from Jesus. A little miracle would be a clear indication he was authentic and speaking in God's name. Jesus told them they would see a sign later. It would be a powerful and universal sign of divine love — his death and resurrection. He would exit the grave, like Jonah leaving the belly of the whale. We call it the paschal mystery and still honor this wonderful sign today. If ever we have doubts about God's love for us, we don't need to ask Him to prove it by some small and often foolish sign. We simply need to remember his death and resurrection for us; it's a sign for all times. It tells of his convincing victory over the grave and his promise to share eternal life with us.

TUESDAY, SIXTEENTH WEEK OF THE YEAR
Ex 14:21 - 15:1 and Mt 12:46-50

In this passage from the book of Exodus, we read a graphic description of God's punishment of the Egyptians. It must be extremely difficult for Egyptian Christians to read and accept these Bible passages today. In our attempt to understand, we want to be sure we imply no racism against Egyptians for they are caring and loving people. The real point being made here is not that God is specifically against Egyptians, but rather that he opposes any person or nation that impedes those who are following his directives. Realizing the varied and hostile backgrounds of Egypt and Israel, we marvel even more at the historical meeting between their leaders: Egypt's Anwar Sadat and Israel's

Menachem Begin a number of years ago. It was a moment of hopefulness when these two came to Washington, D.C. to discuss peace terms with President Jimmy Carter. Jesus here tells his followers to avoid current divisions because of past hostilities and racial backgrounds. Jesus in fact considers those who do his will to be as intimate members of his personal family. He refers to them as brothers and sisters regardless of nationalities or past mistakes. Friendship with God transcends all race, color and former hostilities. It is based on current sincerity of heart.

WEDNESDAY, SIXTEENTH WEEK OF THE YEAR
Ex 16:1-5, 9-15 and Mt 13:1-9

It would seem that since Jesus was preaching from a boat some of his examples and parables in this situation would naturally be from the sea, involving water, fish or storms. Instead he tells a parable about the land — about a farmer sowing seed in his field. Although he is sitting in a boat some yards out from the shore on the sea, the people who hear him are on the land and the Lord always preaches to the people where they are. Jesus reminds the people that the land contains many different kinds of soil, just as those who were listening to him there possess many different kinds of hearts. Some are the hard and stony type. They are skeptical of all they hear and very slow to believe. Seeds can not take root in that type of soil and even God's words can not move those kinds of hearts. There are also the fickle ones. They believe one thing now and something else tomorrow. Some soil also begins to produce wheat but, through neglect, ends up with nothing but weeds. Other hearts are open, receptive and workable. Even so there are degrees of productiveness. God's word (the seed) is capable of producing 100%. The only limiting factor is how we, the soil, respond.

THURSDAY, SIXTEENTH WEEK OF THE YEAR
Ex 19:1-2, 9-11, 16-20 and Mt 13:10-17

God tells Moses, "I am coming to you in a dense cloud." In the cloud were thunder and lightning, which scared the people and made them tremble. The clouds, thunder and lightning were nebulous, formless and mysterious. They evoked fear, faith, prayer, awe and discussion among the people. God was transmitting a message, but it was not totally clear just what was being communicated. In the gospel, Jesus is addressing the crowd and the apostles ask him why he is speaking in parables. Again, the message is given in a mysterious and veiled manner. A parable is open to many different interpretations, and one can grasp the full meaning only through a lot of reflection and faithful prayer. The parables of the New Testament are like the clouds of the Old Testament. We may want to learn of God from books and teachers which will give us clear and certain answers. The reality is that religious answers are not always all that precise and clear. We must untangle God's message from the doubts and confusion which occasionally surround it. Each of us, individually, is invited to learn the how's and why's of life by searching the clouds, listening to the thunder, watching the lightning, and "unpuzzling" the parables. This is the way, Scripture says, that God dealt with the people of the past and continues to communicate with the present generation today.

FRIDAY, SIXTEENTH WEEK OF THE YEAR
Ex 20:1-17 and Mt 13:18-23

Today we are presented with the famous Old Testament passage which sets forth the Ten Commandments in the Book of Exodus, chapter 20. This is the first of two listings of the Ten Commandments; the other is to be found in the Book of

Deuteronomy. These are a mere fraction of the commandments the Hebrew people possessed. General agreement is that there were more than 600 in all. The Ten are highlighted because of the unique manner in which they were given to the people through Moses, and because of their broad spectrum. Jesus came to simplify the commandments and to teach a less entangled code of morality. Although the Old Testament, in a sense, reduced the 600 to 10, Jesus reduced them to two. His statement has become a classic. It calls us to love God with all our heart and soul and strength, and to love our neighbors as ourselves. Notice that the Lord does not say the second is inferior to the first, but like the first. That means loving our neighbor is as important as loving God. Although our neighbor can be difficult to love at times, we are still expected to love him or her just as surely as we are to love our God. It is simply the way to act. Loving God and neighbor to the fullest — which means in some way sacrificing one's life for them — is the summation of all morality.

SATURDAY, SIXTEENTH WEEK OF THE YEAR
Ex 24:3-8 and Mt 13:24-30

It would be a wonderful world if all people in society were honest and kind. That was the way it was envisioned to be in the beginning of creation. Soon evil made its appearance and began to vie with the good. The struggle of our first parents highlighted the difficulties which good has in subduing evil. The struggle continues in our times. Sometimes it appears that evil predominates and that honest and good people are dwindling. All of us have wondered why the sinful often thrive, when the good and innocent face so many hardships. Why doesn't God punish the evil now? Wipe them off the earth? We are made and loved by a gentle and long suffering God. We have all sinned and yet we're not destroyed by God, so others, likewise, are not eliminated when they sin. That is the meaning of the weeds living with the wheat. It is the Christian belief that life itself can be and, in fact, will be very unfair to those who act uprightly. Yet the eternal hope is that all things will end well. In the reality of nature weeds can not become wheat, but in the spiritual realm the sinner can become a saint. Therefore the sinner, who is potentially a holy person, is given time to be converted and find salvation.

MONDAY, SEVENTEENTH WEEK OF THE YEAR
Ex 32:15-24, 30-34 and Mt 13:31-35

Moses descended the famous Mount Horeb where he had been for forty days. He carried with him the two tablets of the Ten Commandments. No doubt, he was extremely happy to have received such a concise and simple format for living which he could present to his people. As he neared the base of the mountain, though, he found the people doing precisely what the first commandment forbade. "Thou shall not have strange gods before me." The people were worshipping an idol and Moses became extremely angry with them. In his deep disappointment and fury, Moses, a holy man of God, broke all Ten Commandments on the spot. We do not carry about with us two stones tablets with the rules of morality inscribed on them as Moses did, but we can still break the commandments. And when we do, God is good and forbearing giving us a chance to begin again. Moses began again by returning to the mountain top and receiving another set of commandments, free of charge. We, literally or figuratively, may have broken all the commandments ourselves and feel most unworthy to return to the presence of God. But, like the Israelites, we must make known to God some way our intention to reform: "We will do everything the Lord has told us." Regardless of how we have broken the commandments, our emphasis must be placed on God who is patient and forgiving and who provides us with the graces and opportunities we need each day to live them.

TUESDAY, SEVENTEENTH WEEK OF THE YEAR
Ex 33:7-11; 34:5-9, 28 and Mt 13:35-43

We speak to God in our many prayers and devotions. God speaks to us in signs and symbols plus through the many inspirations that come into our lives. When the Scriptures say that God spoke to certain people, we tend to think of God as giving inspirations to those individuals rather than as exchanging actual words with them. In the Exodus reading at today's Mass, however, the author says very explicitly that Moses really spoke to God "face to face, as one man speaks to another." This must have been an impressive thing indeed. All the people would stand at the entrances of their tents when this was happening, and the realization of what was taking place moved them to worship God. Through Moses the whole community lived in close associate with the Lord. The prayer of Moses is also very touching as he invites God to come along in their company. For us to live in the presence of God, we must speak with him often in prayer, on the most intimate and personal level possible. In our liturgy we converse with the Lord before we meet him "face to face" in Holy Communion. Like Moses, we should invite God to come along with us on our pilgrimage throughout the day.

WEDNESDAY, SEVENTEENTH WEEK OF THE YEAR
Ex 34:29-35 and Mt 13:44-46

When the sun is shining through stained glass windows, they glow with a lovely brilliance. At night the beauty of the window is reversed. Then the light within makes the window glow and smile on the outside. The grace and love of God glowed within Moses and reflected joy and peace on the outside. When we are filled with loving grace, we can not hide it from others. It will show forth in our faces, eyes, words and tones of voice and in our thoughts. God's grace is first poured into our lives and then our souls reflect it to others in the world. We're very often preoccupied with how we appear externally and the way others look. The real beauty within ourselves and others can easily be ignored. Jesus, brilliant within, appeared rather ordinary on the outside. We catch a fleeting glimpse of his real glory at the transfiguration on the mountain. It so attracted the three apostles that they wanted to stay right there with the Lord forever. External beauty, as we all know, is something which will pass away; only that within will not fade with time. In fact, it is meant to last forever.

THURSDAY, SEVENTEENTH WEEK OF THE YEAR
Ex 40:16-21, 34-38 and Mt 13:47-53

Jesus tells us today that one learned in the ways of God will be able to bring forth from his storeroom both the old and the new. One interpretation of this passage is that the informed Christian will understand the Old Testament as well as the New, and be able to bring them together in such a way as to have a comprehensive understanding of Jesus and his teaching in the fullest possible historical perspective. The Old Testament, or "The Law" as it was often called, must be seen as laying the foundation and preparation for the coming of Christ. The New Testament, or the Good News, can then be better appreciated as we see how it has fulfilled the Old. To understand and appreciate any current reality, we first must know its history. We can not possibly understand the current conflict of the Jews and Arabs, with their hostages and retaliations, without some knowledge of their history. We cannot fully appreciate the current, post Vatican II Church, without knowing the practices before Vatican II and how the changes have attempted to make the message of

Jesus more applicable to modern times. What you and I are to do today, is based on what we were and did yesterday and in former years of our life. The wise person reflects on and understands both the old and new. Such a one is neither a traditionalist nor a progressivist but a realist who is faith-filled.

FRIDAY, SEVENTEENTH WEEK OF THE YEAR
Lv 23:1, 4-11, 15-16, 27, 34-37 and Mt 13:54-58

Rodney Dangerfield has made a good living by playing the role of one who gets no respect. We have all seen him wiping his brow and shaking his head lamenting his sad fate as he humorously recounts situations in which he got no respect from anyone. Many in this world get little or no respect and it's not a very funny situation. People simply ignore others who have fine talents and abilities but, for some reason, are not accepted. Perhaps they don't live in the right sections of town or associate with the right crowd to get accepted. Jesus was a native of Nazareth, yet the people of that small village in Galilee gave him little respect. They were the ones who tried to throw him over a hill and, in today's gospel, they again refuse to believe in the words he speaks. Because of their disbelief, Jesus was unable to work any miracles for them, for a miracle — to some degree — depends on the faith of others. His fellow citizens simply would not take him at his word. There was no way, in their minds, that he could be anyone other than a fellow townsman. Here Jesus declares himself to be a prophet and sees his rejection as a confirmation of his prophetic role. We need to recognize and appreciate the goodness and talent of the members of our own families and of others in our neighborhood and in our community. God may be saying something to us through them. They deserve our respect.

SATURDAY, SEVENTEENTH WEEK OF THE YEAR
Lv 25:1, 8-17 and Mt 14:1-12

Today's reading from the book of Leviticus explains a very ancient and unique practice in Israel. Seven was a sacred number and seven times seven was extremely holy. So after seven times seven years, there was to be a holy year of rest. This would, therefore, occur every 50 years. Not only was this a time for human rest, but the fields were also to lie fallow and no crops were to be planted in them that year. Besides this aspect of rest, and even more dramatic, was the practice of releasing prisoners and forgiving debts. These and other merciful and reconciling deeds were likewise to be performed. With good reason, this 50th year was called a "Jubilee Year." Currently the State of Israel is in the final seven year period since the establishment of their country in 1948. What a wonderful thing it would be if Israel were to celebrate its Jubilee Year in 1997 by releasing hostages and forgiving the hurts and misgivings of the past. Just imagine the universal goodwill which could be generated by such a gesture! If that were ever to take place, it would truly be a Jubilee Year for the entire world to celebrate. We too, as individuals, can and should declare our own Jubilee years, preparing ourselves for them by doing something of a merciful and forgiving nature, as would befit a true follower of Jesus.

MONDAY, EIGHTEENTH WEEK OF THE YEAR
Nb 11:4-15 and Mt 14:13-21

The Hebrews slaves in Egypt desperately wanted freedom, but when they achieved their new found freedom, they soon began to complain about all the difficulties it involved. They had to realize that freedom did not come free. To preserve it they would have to endure hunger, thirst, long marches and other unforeseen hardships. When these became a reality, they started to complain against Moses for bringing them out into the desert to die of starvation. They longed for the cucumbers, melons, onions and garlic of Egypt. It was because of their bitter complaining that they received the manna, which fell from heaven with the dew. The manna had the taste of coriander seed, which was a herb grown in the ancient world, with a carrot-like taste. It was also described as being bdellium, that is a resin or gum-like substance. So the manna must have tasted something like carrot flavored bubble gum. This was transition-food and the time in the desert was a time of purification. It was the price of freedom. During World War II, the U.S. military served "Spam" to all the soldiers. It was something most didn't really relish, but it was their war time diet. The Lord feeds us at Mass with a new "manna" from heaven. It's food for the road. We prayerfully appreciate all our blessings and freedoms and gladly endure the costs necessary to make freedom lasting.

TUESDAY, EIGHTEENTH WEEK OF THE YEAR
Nb 12:1-13 and Mt 14:22-36

When we find ourselves in precarious situations and become frightened, we can cry out in prayer, as St. Peter did: "Lord save me." And we can expect Jesus to stretch out his hand to uplift us, lest we sink beneath the raging waves. That is the tender and beautiful scene which is presented in today's gospel. When we have broken trust with the Master and sinned, we may feel rejected and about to sink beneath our problems and sorrows. Then we can cry out: "Lord save me." And again we can expect to find the uplifted and forgiving hand of Jesus, catching us in the middle of the sea. The Lord will assist us into the boat we thought we had missed, and all will become calm and peaceful when only moments before we thought we were on the verge of perishing.

These are the times and situations in life when we are moved to respond to the Lord with the heartfelt words of St. Peter: "Undoubtedly, you are the Son of God!" Can we begin walking toward the Lord without fear, with little or no support beneath our feet? Peter stepped out in faith and if he would just have kept his mind and eyes on Jesus and forgotten about the high winds and deep sea, he would have walked the distance with ease. Whether on water or dry land, strong faith enables us to move unfalteringly toward Jesus.

WEDNESDAY, EIGHTEENTH WEEK OF THE YEAR
Nb 13:1-2, 25 - 14:1, 26-29, 34-35 and Mt 15:21-28

This gospel passage is the story of a woman who refused to take "no" for an answer. We often hear it said that all prayers are answered but sometimes the answer is "no." This Canaanite woman would not believe that statement. The implication here is that Jesus and his apostles are taking a short break from the ministry and traveling outside their country. The last thing they needed was another person begging for a miracle. It's amazing that this foreigner even recognized Jesus. Our Lord here is influenced by his apostles, for they tell him to send her away and Jesus tries to. Notice that she doesn't come to Jesus through the apostles, but directly. She matches Jesus quip for quip and is not offended at some rather harsh statements made against her. To get angry or be offended would have defeated her cause. She was determined to get a cure for her daughter and, in spite of all odds, she accomplished what she set out to do. Jesus does a complete about-face with her — from saying she is none of his concern to praising her for her fantastic faith and then healing her daughter. This is one of the classic Scripture stories of perseverance. Even if Jesus treats us like a dog, we can remember, there are still some crumbs for us on the Master's table.

THURSDAY, EIGHTEENTH WEEK OF THE YEAR
Nb 20:1-13 and Mt 16:13-23

This passage from the sixteenth chapter of Matthew has been used to explain many things that we find in the Church: the primacy of Peter, the office of the pope, the forgiveness of sins, etc. On the lighter side, the text explains the "real name" of the first pope. Jesus calls him "Simon, son of John" or Johnson. Then he refers to him as "Rock," or as we would say, Rocky. Therefore, the name of the first pope was "Rocky Johnson." As we know, names of people were often changed to those which would seem more fitting to the new office to which they had been called. Since the name Peter is from the Greek word "petra," it was a very descriptive name for Jesus to give to Simon. The nature of his new office would require him to be solid and strong, like the rock on which the weight of the Church, down through the centuries, would be built. Even though Peter is designated as leader of the others, he, like all the rest, is expected to follow Jesus closely. When Peter tried to dissuade the Lord from pursuing the difficult way the Father had given him, Jesus sharply commanded him to get behind him, not out front. He is to get in line and follow like a true disciple should. We, as disciples of Jesus, are also to walk behind the Lord, for the word disciple means "one who follows." Our names, too, have been changed to fit our spiritual role. From the day we were baptized, we are called "Christians."

FRIDAY, EIGHTEENTH WEEK OF THE YEAR
Dt 4:32-40 and Mt 16:24-28

In this reading from Deuteronomy, Moses tells the people to remember the days of old and people of the past, whom God so loved and cared for. They are to realize that God is the same God and that he loves and will care for the present generation, as surely as he did for their ancestors. God's promises are for ever and, in them, the people are to have tremendous hope for the future. They also are to tell their children of the faithful goodness of God. We, today, constantly recall the life and death of Jesus, remembering we are heirs of his promises. The past builds a road to the future, as we are reminded at each Mass when we again fulfill the Lord's request to "do this in memory of me." When burdensome problems and unsettling questions come marching into our lives, like mighty forces to defeat us, we can and should remember the past when stronger powers were defeated. Moses was filled with awe and admiration for God when he asked: "Did anything so great ever happen before?" We, who are the beneficiaries of the saving deeds of Jesus, have even more reason to be astonished than Moses. Remember, joyfully, all the blessings the Lord Jesus has bestowed in the past and look forward to those he's promised for the future.

SATURDAY, EIGHTEENTH WEEK OF THE YEAR
Dt 6:4-13 and Mt 17:14-20

Anthony was a friend of mine who, during his high school years, was an outstanding distance runner. He was a good student and faithfully prepared for his classes and exams. He also prepared himself for each race by determining beforehand how fast a time he wanted to run. He would often write his desired time on a small piece of paper, which he carried in his pocket. Sometimes it would be inked on his arm, and he said that he even posted it on the headboard of his bed. In this way, his mind and body accepted the challenge beforehand. And, on the track, he normally won. Moses tells the Hebrew people to profess and live the love of God with their entire beings. This wonderful passage is known as the "Shema." Everyone was to keep these ideas fixed firmly in their minds and hearts and souls. He tells the parents to drill them into their children. Speak them at home and on the road. Think of them, whether busy or resting. If that's not enough, he further tells them to tie these sacred words around their wrists and foreheads and write them on the door posts of their home and on the yard gates. When God's love is firmly fixed in our minds and hearts, we can meet any challenge and be crowned a winner.

MONDAY, NINETEENTH WEEK OF THE YEAR
Dt 10:12-22 and Mt 17:22-27

Note that in the first sentence of this reading, Moses tells the Israelite people both to fear and to love God. The two words are used interchangeably. Fear and love do not stand in opposition to each other as we often imagine. A synonym for fear in this context would be reverence or respect. All who respect God and keep the commandments are the friends of God. We don't need to consider if we're doing a particular good deed from a motive of fear or love, since they are similar. When love is very intense there is present the fear of displeasing the one we love. The reading also gives us a wonderful picture of God's fairness, telling us that God has no favorites and accepts no bribes. The word, "terrible," is used here, which we also need to consider in its proper context. The passage says that God that has done "terrible things." If it were said that a person did terrible things we would think that such an individual was an evil person, and ought to be punished by God. Terrible here refers to things that might frighten us, in the sense of things that are awesome, certainly not evil. The whole passage emphasizes how loving, awesome and mysterious God really is.

TUESDAY, NINETEENTH WEEK OF THE YEAR
Dt 31:1-8 and Mt 18:1-5, 10, 12-14

The name of Moses was synonymous with the entire Hebrew nation for many years. He had organized and led the Exodus, had spoken to God in their behalf, presented them with the Ten Commandments and had been the ultimate human word regarding advice and regulations. It was time now for Moses to step aside, for he was 120 years old and a younger man, Joshua, would henceforth be in charge. It would be Joshua who would lead the people across the Jordan River into the Promised Land. Moses, the excellent leader that he was, saw to the transition of power in such a way that the people gladly accepted Joshua as their new leader. Joshua was publicly approved by Moses as he instructed all the people to continue to be brave, for God would still be marching with them. This might serve as a fine model for the changing of pastors in our parishes. It would be good to see the leaving pastor and the newly appointed one, together, in the sanctuary in the presence of the congregation, like Moses and Joshua. "Moses" could introduce the people to "Joshua" with love and affirmation, encouraging them to accept him and to continue walking with the Lord under their new leader. It would make the transition much easier for everyone involved.

WEDNESDAY, NINETEENTH WEEK OF THE YEAR
Dt 34:1-12 and Mt 18:15-20

There is exhibited here a certain peaceful resignation about the journey of life, and following the will of God. It was decreed in God's wisdom that Moses' life should be spent leading the people to the Jordan, but not crossing over. The river served as both a natural and spiritual boundary of this man's journey. God is considerate of Moses, letting him view from afar the Promised Land which he dreamed of for so many years. Then Moses knew his mission was complete and he was perfectly content to die. We note how Joshua was immediately accepted by the people, since Moses had laid his hands upon him with his departing blessing. Joshua could then begin functioning immediately in preparing the people for the next exciting phase of their national life — the crossing of the Jordan River. No jealousy or resentment seems to be present, since all was done with charity and class. Moses continues to be held in the highest esteem as thirty days of mourning are accorded to him. When we are properly motivated — without envy or pride — charity and peace can reign supreme.

THURSDAY, NINETEENTH WEEK OF THE YEAR
Jos 3:7-10, 11, 13-17 and Mt 18:21 - 19:1

Today, we have the second account of God stopping a river so the people can cross over. The first was the Red Sea and now it's the Jordan River. The first was stopped so that the people could exit Egypt with Moses; the second, so that they could enter the Holy Land with Joshua. The water was at flood stage, but it halted when the "priestly bearers of the Ark waded into the water." The water upstream backed up into a lake, while the rest continued down stream and disappeared like the caboose on a speeding freight train. These biblical river-crossings were dangerous situations, but God was there to assist his people. We have our rivers and barriers to cross, our hardships to face and we, too, seek God's assistance. During these difficult times we often turn to prayer, the sacraments, Scripture reading and a dependence on our faith. Since the flowing water can be stopped, we pray that God will halt the flowing pain and dam up all our hurting; that he will stop the flow of blood in the wounded; that he will reverse the tide of hate in the angry and fear in the oppressed. These are our rivers and we need our God's assistance if they are to be crossed.

FRIDAY, NINETEENTH WEEK OF THE YEAR
Jos 24:1-13 and Mt 19:3-12

Divorce is a major modern-day problem which has a long history. Even Jesus was at a loss as to what to do about it. The key is to understand the meaning of being two in one and joined by God. For "two to be as one" means much more than sexual union. In the past, as today, it is evident that many marriages have taken place between the wrong people and for the wrong reasons. Being two in one means a thinking in unison with a common purpose; a mental and spiritual more than a physical bonding. Think of the marriages which have taken place to strengthen a political alliance, to finalize a business deal, or so often to "solve" a delicate situation such as pregnancy. The vows are precise and explicitly stated to give assurance that those who make them are truly — physically, mentally, and spiritually — two in one, and God is joining them together. I heard a joke about a man who lived in the wilderness and advertised for a wife. "She must be able to sew, cook, clean, raise children, to fish and have a motor boat; which she must bring with her." His name and address were given. Then he wrote, "P.S. Send picture of boat and motor." That appears to be a business deal, not an everlasting marriage covenant made by God.

SATURDAY, NINETEENTH WEEK OF THE YEAR
Jos 24:14-29 and Mt 19:13-15

Our daily liturgical readings give very little of the life and deeds of Joshua. Today we have his final address to the people. He reflects over the past history of the nation, about the many things which happened "beyond the River," i.e., on the other side of the Jordan. For those young people who had not travelled with them from Egypt and through the two miraculous river-crossings, he recalls those momentous events. All this is meant to deepen and increase their trusting faith in God. Joshua threatens his followers that if they turn away from serving their true God and follow false gods, that God will punish them. In unison, all pledge to be faithful. Joshua dies at 110, giving him 10 years less life than Moses. A stone is then designated and blessed as a memorial witness to these promises of faithfulness which the people have made. As Christians we, too, glory in the past deeds done for us by Jesus. Daily, we recall and reenact those wonderful works which brought us salvation. A stone or rock, which is the Church, was designated to be a perpetual reminder of all that we have spiritually inherited.

MONDAY, TWENTIETH WEEK OF THE YEAR
Jg 2:11-19 and Mt 19:16-22

The Book of Judges bridges the years between Joshua and Samuel. It likewise spans the time in Israel's history between the repossession of their original land and the establishment of the monarchy. These happenings would most likely have occurred in the 12th and 11th centuries B.C. The judges were not people who presided over court trials, but rather were more like popular and charismatic leaders. They continually emphasized the observance of the law, especially God's commands to avoid idolatry. Repeatedly the people fell away from the God of their ancestors who had delivered them from their slavery in Egypt. They worshipped instead the lesser gods of their pagan neighbors. The judges, realizing that the law is necessary not only for policing but for teaching, threatened the people with God's punishment if the law were not observed. When preachers today proclaim the meaning and spirit of God's law, exhorting the people to adhere to it and even threatening punishment if they do not, it is nothing new. There is a need in our world for people who will remind us of our many past blessings and our need to be faithful to those values originally taught in our churches and upheld by our society. Our history helps to explain our present.

TUESDAY, TWENTIETH WEEK OF THE YEAR
Jg 6:11-24 and Mt 19:23-30

An angel is sent from God to greet the young judge, Gideon, with the words: "The Lord is with you." Gideon replies that if God is with us, why are we being persecuted and suffering so much pain? We ask those same kinds of questions today. The signs we see around us often seem to indicate that God is not with us and does not love us. We say this because of the negative way we often interpret the signs. From his many past deeds and words, there is indisputable evidence, though, that God truly is with us. We should rely on these past deeds and words rather than on the way we might otherwise be inclined to interpret certain current signs and happenings. The most convincing signs of God's eternal love for all people are the Lord's death and resurrection made present to us each day in the Eucharist. These are more convincing than the fire from the rock which Gideon witnessed. May the confusions, discouragements and mysteries of today not cause us to doubt God's presence with us and his abiding love for us. In the Eucharist, the Lord has given us an eternal pledge of his fidelity which is clear, certain and forever.

WEDNESDAY, TWENTIETH WEEK OF THE YEAR
Jg 9:6-15 and Mt 20:1-16

This gospel passage is a parable. It is not a blueprint on how to conduct a wage dispute between management and labor. It's a commentary on God's abiding love and mercy for all people, regardless of their various extenuating circumstances. Some people have been faithful, lifetime followers of God, consistently working in the vineyard. Others have found their way to God only late in life. The point is that all receive the same stipend. We are not paid a wage for serving God. It's all a free-will gift. Since the gift is eternal life, how could one be given more eternal life than another? St. Augustine, who delayed his conversion to Christ as long as possible, remarked afterwards: "Late have I loved you." If we are among the late-comers to be serious about loving and serving God, then we should especially appreciate this parable. The story of God's love and mercy towards people has been told in many ways. The conclusion is always the same: God's love is unlimited and all inclusive. And how fortunate that is for each of us!

THURSDAY, TWENTIETH WEEK OF THE YEAR
Jg 11:29-39 and Mt 22:1-14

This story of the wedding banquet is another parable. Especially intriguing is the ending, which is also somewhat disturbing. But remember, parables often exaggerate in one area in order to make a specific point in another. The person is dismissed from the banquet, not because of the external clothes he is wearing, but for his lack of internal disposition. It speaks to the question of those who try to enter the kingdom without any basis in faith. How do we get ready for church? We shouldn't be thinking only about what clothes we will wear. When coming to the banquet of the Eucharist, our primary consideration should concern what we will wear next to our heart — our faith. If we come to the banquet without faith, we are not spiritually dressed in the proper attire. We really don't belong. We can be invited to attend and also invited to leave, as are the present-day catechumens in the RCIA Program. This symbolizes that those who are not yet in full communion may share in the liturgy of the word, but not in the eucharistic banquet until they achieve full membership. Do we come into the presence of God with the right dispositions?

FRIDAY, TWENTIETH WEEK OF THE YEAR
Rt 1:1, 3-6, 14-16, 22 and Mt 22:34-40

This Old Testament passage from the Book of Ruth is often read at wedding ceremonies. Especially impressive are verses 16 and 17 in chapter one. "Do not ask me to abandon or forsake you! For wherever you go I will go, wherever you lodge I will lodge, your people shall be my people and your God shall be my God. Wherever you die I will die, and there be buried." Tender as it is, the original setting of the passage was not a wedding at all. The words were not even exchanged between a man and woman, but between a young widow and her mother-in-law. This quality caring is presented as an ideal kind of love, which should be present in all of us. The passage sets the stage for the more solemn words of the gospel. Here Jesus summarizes the entire moral law in the two commandments of love: loving God with one's whole heart and soul and mind and one's neighbor as oneself. There are a million ways to relate to God and to others, but Scripture says if that relationship is not steeped in selfless love, it's not the right kind.

SATURDAY, TWENTIETH WEEK OF THE YEAR
Rt 2:1-3, 8-11; 4:13-17 and Mt 23:1-12

The "what ifs" of history can make our heads spin with wonderment. What if Ruth, the Moabite woman, would have decided to return to her own people after her husband's death, as her sister-in-law, Orpah, did? What if, when after Ruth and

Naomi had returned to Bethlehem, Naomi's home, Ruth would have looked for food in a field other than the one belonging to Boaz? Scripture says that it was quite by chance that she went to the field of Boaz, rather than to another. Life's possibilities are countless. The reality here is that Ruth married Boaz. Their son, Obed, became the father of Jesse and Jesse became the father of King David. The lives of our ancestors are filled with a lot of "what ifs" also. With one small change of events our grandparents or parents may not have met or married and we would never have existed. Our faith testifies that we are here not by pure chance, but because of God's providence. Every person who exists on this earth today is the visible result of millions of past decisions, back through the centuries of time. And God, somehow, was involved in the consequences of all those decisions. As a result, there is in each of us a high dignity and a lasting value.

MONDAY, TWENTY-FIRST WEEK OF THE YEAR
1 Th 1:2-5, 8-10 and Mt 23:13-22

For the next eight days the first reading, in the weekly lectionary, will be from Paul's first letter to the Thessalonians. This letter has the distinction of being the earliest writing of the New Testament. Paul is elated that the people in Thessalonica have received the gospel of Jesus and are living it with much conviction. That Greek community did two things for which Paul was very grateful. First, they accepted him, and were willing to listen to his message. Second, they took Paul's preaching very seriously, and turned from idols to serve the true God. Idol worship was a major problem among the people at that time. Many, though, were so impressed by the Christian message that they abandoned their worship of idols. Not only did they learn from Paul, but he received a new insight into the power of the Holy Spirit which made these changes in their lives. Even their neighbors were impressed and told others. We can imitate those early Thessalonians by listening carefully each time we hear the Scriptures read and by continuing to be converted from the sinful "idols" in our lives. In such a way, we, too, testify to the fact that God's message is not mere words, but the power of the Spirit.

TUESDAY, TWENTY-FIRST WEEK OF THE YEAR
1 Th 2:1-8 and Mt 23:23-26

When we hear certain people speaking enthusiastically on some topics, we often become skeptical. They may impressively explain how a certain food, gadget or investment will benefit our lives, but we still are hesitant to believe. If the people are from out of town, who are trying to sell us something, we are even more skeptical. Paul implies that same practice was prevalent in his day. The out-of-towners would try to deceive the people and sway them to their point of view, through trickery and flattering words or whatever would help them make a sale. Here Paul gives reassurance to the Thessalonians that he is one "out-of-towner" who is not trying to trick them for some kind of personal gain. Although he comes from Tarsus in Asia Minor, which is 800 miles away, he can be trusted and believed. Paul reminds them that even though he and his companions hold important positions in the Church, he minimized that aspect lest the people be manipulated in any way. He is believed because he is not promoting himself, but Jesus the Lord.

WEDNESDAY, TWENTY-FIRST WEEK OF THE YEAR
1 Th 2:9-13 and Mt 23:27-32

Recently a weather man on TV explained the meaning of the term, "the doldrums." Doldrums cause the weather to happen.

Located over the water at the equator, these high thick masses of clouds instigate the various weather patterns that affect the entire world. It takes many days for these numerous weather patterns to reach their destination, but eventually they arrive. Our inner dispositions are like those cloud-shrouded doldrums. Our happiness or depression today may be traced back to something which happened days ago, but whose effects are just now manifesting themselves in us. In this passage, Paul pleads with the Thessalonians to make their lives worthy of Christ. God's influence in our lives will help us to live more worthy of Christ. Some kind words or deeds spoken or done years ago may, in days yet to come, inspire us or others to extend equally kind words and deeds to another. The many kindnesses extended to each of us over the years should encourage us to be more kind and considerate to others whom we may encounter today.

THURSDAY, TWENTY-FIRST WEEK OF THE YEAR
1 Th 3:7-13 and Mt 24:42-51

Many events occur without any warning or announcement. I'll long remember the anguish on the faces and in the voices of an elderly couple, whose home had been vandalized by several young men and then set on fire and burned to the ground. This happened while the couple was on vacation — only the second vacation they had ever taken in their many years of marriage. "If only we had stayed home," they kept saying, "this wouldn't have happened." Evil and hurt can come into our lives very unexpectedly but so can blessings. The fact of the matter is that blessings come much more frequently. They come so often we don't even recognize them. They are simply taken for granted. Our hearts are still beating, the sun rises, food tastes good, we have a job, family, happiness, hope for the future and millions of other, often over-looked, gratuities. Jesus tells us in this gospel to stay awake and alert for the coming of the Lord, for the Lord will come with a hand full of blessings at a time we least expect. Be conscious of God coming into your life today and expect good things to happen. Prepare yourself for his inspirations and his blessings.

FRIDAY, TWENTY-FIRST WEEK OF THE YEAR
1 Th 4:1-8 and Mt 25:1-13

Paul is the image of a man constantly on the go, a person not allowing himself time to relax. His missionary journeys, preaching and writing appears to have been a full-time job. Inwardly also he was busy, ever attempting to deepen his spirituality. In this letter to the Thessalonians, Paul tries to ignite them with the same spirit which he possessed. He tells them that they have learned much about pleasing God, which they are doing. That's fine. But he adds, "you must learn to make still greater progress." The progress he recommends is similar to what he will later suggest to the Colossians: that they grow in love of God and neighbor. Then he mentions what will keep us from this growth in holiness. Sexual immorality, he says, will prevent a person from spiritual development. Today we live in a sex-saturated society. Sexual activities of every kind are now considered routine and common place. Many practices, unthinkable a few years ago, are now taken for granted. Often this new sexual license leads to increased violence, especially against women. The use of drugs nowadays, for a "quick fix" and a real "high," has moved into first place, even ahead of sex. What kind of exotic pleasures will eventually surpass the use of drugs? We, like the Thessalonians, must learn to make greater spiritual progress if we're to truly live. That's the ultimate high.

SATURDAY, TWENTY-FIRST WEEK OF THE YEAR
1 Th 4:9-12 and Mt 25:14-30

This parable is an exhortation for all people to use the gifts which are given to them. How much each person possesses is not the point. The main question is, "How do we use our gifts, whether they are many or few?" The master in the story, from a financial perspective, did very well from his money arrangements. He left town with $5,000.00 "invested" and returned home to find this amount had increased to $15,000.00. The focus of this story centers on those who had acted as stock brokers. We wonder what commodities the two invested in to obtain their 100% interest. The master's anger is directed against the third who invested in nothing and made 0% interest. Whatever gifts we are handed, they are not for our private use alone. They are also intended for the glory of God and the service of our neighbor. Jesus used his divine and unique talents to found the Church and bring salvation to the world, by dying on the cross and rising from the tomb. Every gift has a deeper purpose and a higher goal. Have we used our talents well?

MONDAY, TWENTY-SECOND WEEK OF THE YEAR
1 Th 4:13-18 and Lk 4:16-30

It's often debated if Jesus clearly knew the meaning of his mission when he was born, or if he became aware of it only as he matured. Regardless of which view we accept, the Lord is seen in today's reading as being fully aware of who he is and what he is called to do. Jesus knew exactly what passage he wanted to read in the synagogue. He deliberately unrolled the scroll until he found it. When he finished reading it, the Lord said very openly that this passage from Isaiah referred to him. In the next few years, Jesus actually accomplished what Isaiah had indicated. It is a clear statement of the Lord's mission and must have been one of his favorite passages. Do we have a passage of Scripture that describes our mission in life? If we were to choose one, which would we select? If we, like Jesus, could truly believe the Spirit of God is upon us, we could be more inspired by God and accomplish much good. What a unique sense of renewed purpose we would have, if we could see our lives fulfilling a scriptural passage. There are so many fine choices. We should select one by which to live.

TUESDAY, TWENTY-SECOND WEEK OF THE YEAR
1 Th 5:1-6, 9-11 and Lk 4:31-37

It's an ancient practice in the Church to pray the vesper prayers before the coming of night fall. This spiritual exercise prepares us for the daily arrival of darkness, which is often associated with fear and danger. We don't want the night to catch us by surprise. Paul describes the suddenness with which Jesus will come, with the image of a thief coming at night. It doesn't mean that the Lord will come at night, but that the Lord will come with dispatch. This whole lesson is a contrast between day and night, alertness and sleep, good and evil. The apostle says that Christians must walk through the night and darkness, like anyone else, but we are not to belong to the darkness. The darkness and the unsavory deeds often associated with night are not to control us. We are to walk in the light. Paul also encourages the people to be sober. Don't say, "the day is done, so I'll get drunk." Think rather, this night is the beginning of tomorrow. I must be ready to make it a success. Bidding someone, "Good night," means more than saying good-bye. It's a wish you'll be protected, free from fear, sober, have God's blessing and a peaceful sleep. Have a good night!

WEDNESDAY, TWENTY-SECOND WEEK OF THE YEAR
Col 1:1-8 and Lk 4:38-44

The Scriptures tell us that Jesus had many days that began early and ended late. In today's passage, Luke follows Jesus from worshipping in the synagogue to Simon's home in Capernaum, where he healed Simon's mother-in-law. Then it was suppertime and she prepared the meal. After supper, as the sun began to set, a massive crowd of sick, crippled and possessed people were at the door waiting to be healed. Everyone there received personal attention for it is stated, ". . . he laid hands on *each* of them and cured them." Early the next morning, the Lord was on his way out of town. He must have left before anyone was awake, for no one saw him leave. The disciples had to go in search of him. Jesus was already in the open country when they found him and he was not about to turn back, for he had more work to do than time in which to do it. What drove him on at such a pace? His own words tell us: ". . . because that is why I was sent." He could not remain long with any one group, as they often requested, for he was sent for all people. Today we come seeking Jesus. We find him in the word, the bread and in each other. We ask the Lord if he will stay with us. He replies: "I will be with you always."

THURSDAY, TWENTY-SECOND WEEK OF THE YEAR
Col 1:9-14 and Lk 5:1-11

Paul tells the Greek people living in Colossae that they should strive to gain "full knowledge" of God's will. Then they will have wonderful "spiritual insight." Their deep knowledge of God's will, he says, will enable them to stand fast — to be secure in their beliefs. The other blessing that comes from knowledge of God is: they will be equipped to endure whatever comes in their lives. Not only will they endure, they shall do so joyfully. These

Scriptures promise that we will enjoy good mental health and spiritual strength once we acquire this "full knowledge" of God. This we do through prayer, study, reading and personal reflection. Knowledge leads to insight, which is a comprehensive understanding of the inner nature of things. Insight enables us to function energetically, for with it we have motives and reasons for what we do. Our knowledge of God affects our personal beliefs which, in turn impact on our spiritual way of life. I have a favorite definition of spirituality: Spirituality is faith raised to a lifestyle.

FRIDAY, TWENTY-SECOND WEEK OF THE YEAR
Col 1:15-20 and Lk 5:33-39

I remember what a startling revelation it was the day I learned that people reach a point in life when they cease growing physically. I was about six years old and my aunt, who lived with us, was going to order a new pair of shoes from the catalog. She wrote the size on the order form without measuring her feet. Whenever I or my brothers ordered shoes, we always had to measure our feet first. I asked my mother why my aunt didn't do that. She explained that people reach a certain age and then they and their feet stop growing. That was news to me. The new wine, like the young body, grows and expands rapidly. The skin must grow and stretch also. When fermentation has been completed, it stops expanding. The old wine, like the older body, does not expand but continues to grow in dignity. The older wine is the better. Even though we stop growing physically, we are expected to keep growing constantly in other ways — intellectually, socially and spiritually. Today we assemble in this religious setting to grow in love with our God and with each other. Whether we bubble as the young or increase in dignity like the old, our spirits should always strive to improve, so that today will always find us better than yesterday.

SATURDAY, TWENTY-SECOND WEEK OF THE YEAR
Col 1:21-23 and Lk 6:1-5

The Old Testament laws concerning Sabbath observance were very strict. These inflexible rules were meant to keep that day very holy. However, like some other Old Testament laws, they went too far in legislating detailed "morality." Originally intended to enhance the quality of life, they became ends in themselves and actually placed the law ahead of peoples' needs. The complaint, in this instance, is not that the apostles were stealing someone else's grain, but that they were doing work on the Sabbath. What else were they to do, being out on the road with Jesus, hurrying to their next mission and being very hungry? Feeding the hungry — both ourselves and others, is a basic need. It takes precedence over a tiny bit of manual labor on the Sabbath. The whole question centers on living by the spirit of the law. All that we should do or avoid cannot be spelled out in detail. That's why we have a brain, a conscience and an obligation to live by them. Jesus recognized that the letter of the law can kill, but the spirit of the law gives life. To understand the law, we must try to distill the original intention of the lawgiver. That will enable us both to appreciate and to live the true spirit of the law.

MONDAY, TWENTY-THIRD WEEK OF THE YEAR
Col 1:24 - 2:3 and Lk 6:6-11

Jesus worked a number of his miracles in the synagogue, as is the case in today's Gospel. This one, like most, was done to help someone who was hurting. How fortunate, for the man with the withered right hand, that he had decided to come to worship on this particular day. This person, unlike some others, did not actively seek a cure. It's interesting to note that Jesus not only spotted his crippled hand but he was aware of the "crippled" minds of the judgmental scribes and Pharisees as well. In full view of all, the Lord caused the man's defective hand to be instantly and perfectly restored. What an unexpected answer to prayer that poor man received. We have come to church today to offer our prayers and praise to God. As the Lord looks at us now, is there anything present within us that needs to be healed? Let's offer that part of our body, mind or soul to the Lord's healing power. Maybe the healing will not be as dramatic or instantaneous as the one recorded in the Bible, but we should expect to find some improvement in at least one of these three areas. Whenever we offer ourselves to the Lord in faith, to some extent we are always blessed and healed.

TUESDAY, TWENTY-THIRD WEEK OF THE YEAR
Col 2:6-15 and Lk 6:12-19

Before selecting the twelve apostles, Luke tells us that Jesus spent the entire night "in communion" with God. In this way, our Lord made a concentrated effort to select twelve men who were the choices of his Father. As he had taught his disciples to seek always and in all things the will of the Father, (When you pray, say Our Father . . . , "Thy will be done"), so he himself also turned to the Father and prayed with those same sentiments on this and many other occasions. Before major decisions we, too, should enter into communion with God. In that way we are leaving the final decision to divine wisdom and in God's hands. I wonder if we have ever spent the entire night in prayer in our effort to make the proper judgment in some important matter. We normally think of "going to communion" when we sacramentally receive the Body of Christ. That, though, is often only a brief encounter. After a rather hasty thanksgiving, we are on our way and our closeness with God is crowded out by other concerns. There is a big difference between going to communion and being in communion. Receiving Holy Communion is excellent and highly recommended. Ideally, though, it should lead us to live in communion with God, throughout the day and night.

WEDNESDAY, TWENTY-THIRD WEEK OF THE YEAR
Col 3:1-11 and Lk 6:20-26

St. Paul lays some heavy spirituality on the people of Colossae in this section of his letter. He tells them to live and think as though they had already died. The Church teaches that, spiritually, we have died and have come back to life with Christ through our baptism. In that sacrament, we died spiritually with Jesus on the cross and rose with Jesus from the grave. Paul says that, therefore, we are to put aside and not be attached to those things which are rooted in the earth. All unnecessary encumbrances should be shed. Physical death reduces us to a common denominator where we lose most of our distinguishing characteristics. In death we are no longer divided from each other by incidentals such as whether we've been circumcised or not, were free or slave in this world, Greek or Jew. Jesus likewise reminds us that death puts us all on the same level, without the divisions we had in this world. In death, there is no longer a distinction between the rich and the poor, members of different races, religious denominations, or nationalities. Death not only eradicates these differences, but unites us all as one in Christ. If we can think in terms of having already died, we can better observe equality and live in daily Christian unity.

THURSDAY, TWENTY-THIRD WEEK OF THE YEAR
Col 3:12-17 and Lk 6:27-38

This text from Colossians is well known, since we hear it so often read at weddings. The tone of the passage is one of love and forgiveness and thus very fitting for a reading at a marriage. However, it is intended primarily for the conduct of the entire community, not only for married couples. Paul addresses the people of Colossae with the words, "God's chosen ones, holy and beloved, . . ." These complimentary words were often applied to Israel in the Old Testament. They emphasize the close bond between God and his people. The Colossians, therefore, are to see themselves as members of the New Israel, living an exemplary Christian life in their community. This little passage of five verses could easily be used as a model for establishing our own Christian community. This is what the faculty members of a Christian school ought to be, "God's chosen ones, holy and beloved." The same could be said of the members of a parish council, a liturgy committee and, in fact, all the members of the parish, living and relating to each other. Can we identify our group by its "kindness, humility, meekness and patience"? Do we "bear with one another, forgive . . . grievances" and bind our lives together in love as we ought? Whatever we do, whether in speech or in action, do we do it in the name of the Lord Jesus, always giving thanks to God the Father through him? This, after all, is our vocation.

FRIDAY, TWENTY-THIRD WEEK OF THE YEAR
1 Tm 1:1-2, 12-14 and Lk 6:39-42

The blind must feel their way through this world or hold the hand of another and trust their eyes. A blind person would have very little faith in following another if that other person were also blind. In painting a ridiculous situation Jesus portrays a blind person leading another person who is also blind. He says they'll both fall into a ditch. It would be even more bizarre to designate a blind person as the leader of a group of people with excellent eyesight. When the Lord gets us thinking about who should lead and who should follow, he is referring to those who are spiritually blind to their own faults. Why is it so easy to see the little faults in the lives of others, while at the same time we miss entirely the more conspicuous faults within ourselves? Jesus says our faults may be glaringly large, like a heavy plank, compared to a tiny speck. How do we manage to see the speck and miss the plank? Jesus tells us that those who do this are hypocrites. The term he uses is a Greek word meaning an actor, and here it refers to one who pretends to possess certain qualities which he or she does not have. Let us ask for the grace of spiritual sight.

SATURDAY, TWENTY-THIRD WEEK OF THE YEAR
1 Tm 1:15-17 and Lk 6:43-49

In his first letter to the young bishop, Paul stresses an important basic truth to Timothy. He wants to get Timothy's undivided attention so that what he is about to say will be understood and believed with all his heart. What is this important truth that is worthy of Timothy's "full acceptance? It is this: Jesus Christ came into the world to save sinners." Because we've heard it so often it doesn't have the same impact on us as it surely would have had on those who heard it for the first time. We probably wouldn't totally agree with Paul's next statement that he, Paul, is the worst of all sinners. Paul, however, sees that as a plus, because then Jesus can extend to him the fullness of his mercy precisely because he is an admitted sinner, and Jesus came to save all sinners. We should not shy away from seeing ourselves as sinners — even big sinners. Sinners are not criminals. Nor are they terribly evil people. Sinners are ordinary people who try to live good lives but sometimes, maybe often, fail either by excess or inadequacy. Sinners are dedicated to the pursuit of virtue but often fall short. Still, they attempt to improve and are willing to try again. Even saints are sinners — sinners who've been forgiven. Rather than deny that we are sinners and that we often sin, it is much better to accept the fact and then open our hearts to the mercy of the Lord.

MONDAY, TWENTY-FOURTH WEEK OF THE YEAR
1 Tm 2:1-8 and Lk 7:1-10

The Roman centurion was in charge of 100 soldiers. That's why he was called a centurion — from the Latin word meaning 100. When a centurion issued an order, it was understood in the Roman army that the order would be executed. You could count on that. Maybe the military personnel would not fulfill the order completely but they would certainly make every effort. Even in today's army there is a tremendous respect given to verbal orders and commands, but the reverence for the spoken word was still greater among the Romans. The spoken commands would come to the centurions from their superiors and they in turn would order the troops to act. The centurion commanded tremendous respect and his orders finally set in motion the plan which had originated from the Supreme Commander. This centurion so trusted the spoken word, he said, that Jesus didn't have to come and stand over or touch his servant in order to cure him. All Jesus needed to do was give the command. If the words were spoken, the centurion knew that the desired result would take place. This man was neither a Jew nor a Christian, but what outstanding faith he had in the word of God. Do we have this centurion's same faith in God's word?

TUESDAY, TWENTY-FOURTH WEEK OF THE YEAR
1 Tm 3:1-13 and Lk 7:11-17

Today's Gospel picks up the story of a young man who had died a few hours earlier. Now all his friends and relatives are on the way to the cemetery for his burial. The situation was especially sad, for his mother was a widow and he was her only son. It was the widow's sorrow that moved Jesus to have pity on the son. No doubt he thought of another scene which would come to pass in a couple of years. That would involve him as the only son, and Mary, his widowed mother. Jesus, here in Naim, gives a preview of what he will later do in Jerusalem. To the mother, he says, "Do not cry." Then to the one who had died: "Young man, I bid you get up." This was the funeral procession which never reached the cemetery, for Jesus intervened and sent them all back home with the gift of renewed life. What will be the name of the city and the circumstances in your case someday? Who will cry most bitterly when you have died? We sincerely live our faith now and trust that Jesus will be present in our funeral procession, to bring consolation to our dear ones and to bid us to rise up with him to eternal life?

WEDNESDAY, TWENTY-FOURTH WEEK OF THE YEAR
1 Tm 3:14-16 and Lk 7:31-35

We're well acquainted with the Apostles Creed, used during the rosary, and the Nicene Creed, prayed in unison at our Sunday liturgies. In Scripture there are contained other creeds and certain fixed formulae that were used in the very early Church. Later they got included in the official texts when the Bible was written. In this passage of the letter to Timothy, we read a brief but beautiful old creed. It contains several clear statements of faith in Jesus. It might even have been an ancient hymn as suggested by some of its structure. But whether sung or spoken, it's a wonderful profession of our belief about the life and nature of Our Lord: "He was manifested in the flesh, vindicated in the Spirit; Seen by the angels; preached among the Gentiles, Believed in throughout the world, taken up into glory." It is both succinct and comprehensive, concerning, as it does, some of the essential qualities and deeds of Jesus? Why not memorize these meaningful words and make the thoughts your own personal creed?

THURSDAY, TWENTY-FOURTH WEEK OF THE YEAR
1 Tm 4:12-16 and Lk 7:36-50

This Gospel presents a clear and convincing narrative about Jesus reading the thoughts of people. He could be totally forgiving of the woman because he could see her wholesome and love-filled sentiments concerning him. He could see her motives were not to entice him for pleasure or pay. In spite of her spotted past, she was now open and genuine. The Pharisee, on the other hand, who appeared upright and wholesome did not have the inner qualities to match his exterior comportment. Jesus read his thoughts and saw there a real lack of love. If we have worthy and wholesome motives, God will see them and treat us accordingly. It's so good to know that the Lord is not influenced by the ways we are perceived by others, but knows us for who and what we truly are. Throughout our lives, we have taken different stands on many issues and have been righteous as well as sinful. Maybe we don't even know who or what we are. Scripture says, however, that God knows us well. The real person is not who and what I was in the past, but who and what I am now.

FRIDAY, TWENTY-FOURTH WEEK OF THE YEAR
1 Tm 6:2-12 and Lk 8:1-3

The old saying is, "Birds of a feather, flock together." We know people by the friends they keep, or so we think. The critics of Jesus called him a law breaker because he associated with people who were possessed, prostitutes and tax collectors. Their judgments were cruel, for they did not distinguish between his chosen associates and those to whom he ministered. The "high class" people avoided him and thus did not really get to know the true motives of Jesus. The Lord in turn often spurned the rich and powerful — the scribes and Pharisees — and chose the common people. And they, in turn, chose him. Most of us today would probably be more like the poor and sinful than the rich and important leaders, so we can feel right at home following in the steps of Jesus. The Lord is accustomed to such as we and understands our ways and weaknesses. No matter what we have done, or how we have failed, we have a place with the Savior. The Responsorial Psalm today sings out: "Happy are the poor in spirit — the kingdom of heaven is theirs."

SATURDAY, TWENTY-FOURTH WEEK OF THE YEAR
1 Tm 6:13-16 and Lk 8:4-15

This parable is addressed to a large crowd. In that crowd, people will hear Jesus in many different ways. Much of what they will hear will depend on what they want to hear, for all are at different stages of development. The seed sown is the same for all. The seed is 100% fertile and capable of germination and growth. Some does and some doesn't and other seed has only partial growth. The results are varied, not because of the seed, but because of the different types of soil. Right now we are hearing God's word. The seed is being sown in our hearts at this moment. You can be hardened because of past hurts or personal sins and don't want anything to do with the Word right now. That's the footpath person. You may have some inclination to turn to Jesus wholeheartedly, but after a brief and weak effort you abandon the whole idea. That's the rocky ground. The briar people are those who have too many other interests on their minds at this time. Others will be open to the Lord, and want to grow in God's love. These are the "good soil people." They openly invite the Lord into their lives. God then enables them to be both happy and productive.

MONDAY, TWENTY-FIFTH WEEK OF THE YEAR
Ezr 1:1-6 and Lk 8:16-18

Light is more effective, when placed up high rather than down on the ground. Our lights around buildings, streets and parking lots are mounted above the area to diffuse the light widely. If situated too low, the very purpose of why the light is there is defeated. When we want something to stand out clearly on a printed page, we highlight it with bright, attention-getting ink. We don't lowlight the passage, but highlight it. In the Gospel today, Jesus tells us to lift our lights up high. Place them on lampstands so people can see the light and thereby see where they are walking. The opposite extreme is to hide the light under a basket. We are lights. God's grace within makes us glow with goodness. When others see that goodness, they become enlightened. Our smiles, kind words and good deeds are all small reflections of God — the one mighty light of the world. If we can help others see more clearly where they are going, or what they are doing, then we are placing our lights on the lampstand and highlighting life. We should try, today, to reflect some light on another's path. When we do that, we are doing God's will.

TUESDAY, TWENTY-FIFTH WEEK OF THE YEAR
Ezr 6:7-8, 12, 14-20 and Lk 8:19-21

It is very consoling to read in this Gospel that God forms a unique bond with those who hear his word and act upon it. Jesus says that these people are as close to him as his mother and other intimate family members. In fact, the people who hear and act upon the words of Jesus do become family members of the Lord. Joseph is not mentioned in this passage or in any other situation in the adult life of Jesus. This inference from silence makes us think that he must have died. Regardless, we know how much Jesus loved his mother and cared for her and it is consoling to know that this same closeness is ours, through faith and good works. It is sometimes a lonely business, trying to live by the word of God. The effort can often leave us discouraged, especially if others are making no attempt to live by them. When feeling in need of support and encouragement, we can remember this Gospel passage, from the eighth chapter of St. Luke. When we need assistance and it doesn't come to us, we might think God has abandoned us. At that time, too, it's good to remember we are part of the family and there are times when even the family must stand outside and wait.

WEDNESDAY, TWENTY-FIFTH WEEK OF THE YEAR
Ezr 9:5-9 and Lk 9:1-6

Luke says Jesus first called the Twelve together and gave them many powers for the ministry. Then the Lord sent them forth to preach and heal. They had certain strict guidelines to observe. They were to travel light, and live from the generosity of the people to whom they ministered. Notice the procedure they were to follow. They were not to announce a scheduled meeting for all interested people and then wait to see who or how many would attend. No, Jesus told them to go out to where the people are. Go into their towns, homes and hearts. They were to go out and find the people rather than wait for the people to come to them. Jesus himself went out among the people, to tell the stories of faith and salvation. Today we are to continue to go out to the people. See where they live, share in their lives, speak the message of hope and tell them of the love of Jesus. This passage is very missionary in nature, and it applies to all Christians. Our missionary field of activity is the environment where we live and work, go to school and recreate. Like the original Twelve, we are to continue "spreading the good news everywhere."

THURSDAY, TWENTY-FIFTH WEEK OF THE YEAR
Hg 1:1-8 and Lk 9:18-22

Herod was very curious to see Jesus. Jesus didn't appreciate his curiosity. Herod, it appeared, was not interested in Jesus for what he taught or thought, but regarded him more as a curious phenomenon. To Herod, Jesus was like a person who did a magic act in a side show. We recall the centurion's story told by Luke in last week's readings. He was not overly curious to see Jesus. He even suggested Jesus not come to his home, but just speak the word and his servant would be healed. The Lord complied. This centurion is a fine person to stand in direct contrast to Herod. The centurion was a man of deep faith, while Herod was motivated by fantasy. Christian people are to be guided by faith, as we attempt to see Jesus. But we, too, must be careful, lest we get caught up in the fantasy aspects of religion. We may fulfill our novenas, nine first Fridays and other favorite devotions, and expect favorable results will automatically happen. That is a kind of fantasy. God does not operate with the certain predictability of a chemical equation. Our little formulas do not program the divine. Thus it's not through curiosity that we find Jesus, but through the eyes of faith.

FRIDAY, TWENTY-FIFTH WEEK OF THE YEAR
Hg 1:15 - 2:9 and Lk 9:18-22

Jesus was praying in seclusion and his disciples asked a question. If he were in seclusion, how could his disciples ask a

question? "Praying in seclusion," here means with friends and
faithful followers — his private prayer group. We pray in seclusion with our family, close friends and with our congregation.
These are the people we love and trust. There should be a close
and trusting bond between people who often worship together.
These are our prayer partners. We probably have only minimal
association with many of them in any other context, except that
we pray together. I often wonder if we appreciate, or even truly
recognize, what a profound trust we are fostering with our praying community. In the prayer group of Jesus, there were the
apostles and others who knew the true identity of Jesus. With
these people, the Lord could be himself and be at peace. Can we
see all the members of our church as prayer partners? Do we
have an even closer and smaller group, or one individual with
whom we can pray well and truly be ourselves?

SATURDAY, TWENTY-FIFTH WEEK OF THE YEAR
Zc 2:5-9, 14-15 and Lk 9:43-45

Many of our conversations are idle. We often respond to the
topics set by others, and politely listen, while they expound. Our
interjections of "Yes," "No," "You're right there," "That's the
way it goes," etc., don't give testimony to any strong, inner
convictions on our parts. When we have something interesting to
discuss, people will want to listen and provide meaningful responses. That's the case in the Gospel today. Jesus dramatically
says, "Pay close attention to what I tell you." A preface like that
will quiet the room and people will want to hear. One of the older
translations is: "Lay these words within your ears." This is the
second time Jesus says that he'll be handed over to evil people and
subjected to a most violent death. That's what he wanted the
people to hear. The Lord knew what kind of death he would
endure. He lived with the thought every day. We hope for a

peaceful death and often pray for it. A question often asked the family at a funeral is: "Did the deceased suffer much?" Jesus not only suffered to the extreme at his death, but had to endure suffering everyday of his life since he knew the way he would die. Imagine all the many kind and loving things Jesus did and said, while all the time he was aware of his approaching violent death.

MONDAY, TWENTY-SIXTH WEEK OF THE YEAR
Zc 8:1-8 and Lk 9:46-50

Here Luke records a profound statement of Jesus which can serve as a dependable guideline for our modern day ecumenism. The statement was elicited from Jesus following a comment by John, who had tried to prohibit someone from casting out devils in the name of Jesus, "because he was not of our company." The response of Jesus is recorded by both Mark and Luke: "Do not stop him, for anyone who is not against you is on your side." This is an excellent directive to follow when wondering if we should support and encourage, or at least not resist someone of another religious denomination. Notice the tone here is not just to tolerate, but actively encourage anyone who is doing deeds which promote goodness. The scope of this quote can also be extended to many other situations outside of religion. Anyone, in fact, who is contributing to a better world and a more peaceful society, should have our support. The text can be seen as applying to people in all segments of society. Everyone working for the betterment of society in anyway is not our competitor, but companion, and deserving of our support.

TUESDAY, TWENTY-SIXTH WEEK OF THE YEAR
Zc 8:20-23 and Lk 9:51-56

Jesus was on his way to Jerusalem. How differently the various people understood that phrase, "going to Jerusalem."

The apostles may have viewed it as a change of pace, as a going from the rural setting of Galilee to the big city. The Samaritans protested because here was another group of Jewish people travelling through their territory. The trip to Jerusalem for Jesus was most painful inwardly, for he knew that he was going to suffer and die. The coldness and rejection of the Samaritans did not bother him much. He accepted it as the product of national or racial prejudice and not as something personal. When James and John wanted to make a major issue over the rejection, Jesus reprimanded them. This was not the vicious hatred he would encounter in Jerusalem. But even there the Lord would not "call down fire from heaven to destroy them." Along our road to Jerusalem, we will encounter a world full of people with a variety of attitudes toward us. Different responses will be called for in different circumstances. We, like Jesus, are on a peace mission and non-violence is to be our response to the little hurts and rejections we may encounter along the way. We must avoid thoughts of revenge and continue with our mission.

WEDNESDAY, TWENTY-SIXTH WEEK OF THE YEAR
Ne 2:1-8 and Lk 9:57-62

When you plough a field, especially in strip-farming where there are no ready-made boundaries to follow, you must keep looking ahead. If you continually look back, the furrow is going to be crooked. It will be crooked for all to see, for there is no way you can unplough a field. The disciples are to follow Jesus. Indeed, that is the root meaning of the word disciple. In order to follow, they must keep looking ahead. They are not to look back continually to the Old Testament for guidance and direction. That is now past and the new is at hand. Many of the old religious laws, Jesus says, are now passe. He speaks of them as being dead. Those who want to adhere to them are spiritually dead. So the spiritually dead can bury the physically dead. The disciples are to be the ones who are spiritually alive. They are not to be restricted to any one certain place. They are to have no particular lairs or nests, as do the foxes and the birds, but they must be on the road and available to the needs of the moment. They have a whole wide world to save. Today I will plough another furrow and plant a seed. I'll not look back in fear, remembering past mistakes, but ahead in faith, as I strive to follow Jesus.

THURSDAY, TWENTY-SIXTH WEEK OF THE YEAR
Ne 8:1-4, 5-6, 7-12 and Lk 10:1-12

Jesus appointed seventy-two disciples for the purpose of helping people both hear and accept his teachings. Their assistance was needed, not for some future date after Jesus had ascended into heaven, but during the time he was here in the flesh. They worked in pairs to give support and companionship to each other. Imagine what tremendous results could be achieved if our churches, each day, would send out seventy-two Christian believers to work in the community. These teams of disciples could show the poor how they can be spiritually rich and convey to those in the inner-city that there is hope. Our thirty-six pairs of disciples could comfort the dying with the message that in the other world they will have another opportunity to live. The public, in general, could find encouragement in the wonderful messages found in Psalm 19, which we use in today's liturgy. How happy some would be to hear modern-day disciples speak of God's law refreshing the soul. The world could be led to understand that God's wisdom comes to those with open minds and that lasting joy can be found in right living. We have millions of Christian people out in society each day, but the world doesn't seem to be improving. Could you speak something of Jesus to your friends at work? Jesus sends us today to bring a message of peace and goodwill to others.

FRIDAY, TWENTY-SIXTH WEEK OF THE YEAR
Ba 1:15-22 and Lk 10:13-16

The Word of God is more than a word or a series of words. It is a promise, a covenant and a way of life. It's unique and sacred and we are expected to believe in its lasting value. Jesus had spent much time preaching in the towns of Chorazin and Bethsaida, but the people gave little evidence of being changed in their ways of thinking and acting. In essence, Jesus says in this passage that he is not teaching these people just because he likes to preach, or to entertain them, or to simply fill the time of day. The Lord is preaching to them, and to us, so we will: (1) listen intently to what is said; (2) Remember and reflect on what we have heard; (3) Adjust our thinking to his truths; and (4) Let our actions show evidence that we have been changed. Tyre and Sidon did not change much, but they were Gentile cities. More was expected of the Jewish cities of Bethsaida, Chorazin and Capernaum. They had been prepared in the past and now had no excuse. Try to carry away from each liturgy a new thought from the Word of God. Explore it within yourself and see how it can lead you to a fuller life in Jesus.

SATURDAY, TWENTY-SIXTH WEEK OF THE YEAR
Ba 4:5-12, 27-29 and Lk 10:17-24

We have here the preaching of Jeremiah, as it was dictated to his faithful secretary, Baruch, who committed it to writing. Thus Baruch enabled it to be preserved for succeeding generations. The contents of this passage chides the people for their unfaithfulness to God. That's why they were punished. They were not destined for destruction, but were sent into exile only to teach them a lesson on account of their disobedience to God. The people he is addressing are those of the diaspora, i.e., those

Jewish communities in exile. This passage, which is typical of the entire book, deals with the national guilt of the people of Israel. They had broken their sacred covenant with God and their being conquered and sent into exile were seen as a punishment from God. We, as private citizens, often recall our personal guilt, but how many of us ever take upon ourselves any of the national guilt of the U.S.A. It's easy to say that it's not our responsibility, that it belongs to the Federal Government and other national leaders. We as citizens, though, have a very real obligation, too, to promote the national good as well as our own. We are each responsible for our own personal guilt, and we also share to some degree in the sins of our country.

MONDAY, TWENTY-SEVENTH WEEK OF THE YEAR
Jon 1:1 - 2:1, 11 and Lk 10:25-37

Many things take place in this world which we can not understand. Since we don't understand them, it would be both dishonest and futile to attempt a logical explanation. Instead of trying to give an answer, people have often told stories to shed light on different situations. Stories are also often invented in order to teach a certain lesson. The Bible is full of them. They are called parables. This was a favorite technique used by Jesus. Today we have the parable of the Good Samaritan, a parable which we have heard many times. Now, what we might not understand is that the first reading of today's Mass is also a made-up story or parable. In fact, the entire Book of Jonah is a type of parable. For the next three days in our liturgy, we will read it. As you listen to the selections from the Book of Jonah, don't try to make logical sense out of everything you hear. Simply try to grasp the general principles, and the major truths, which are being taught. Some of these are: (1) We are to do God's will; (2) We are to forgive our enemies; (3) We are expected to be sorry for our sins.

TUESDAY, TWENTY-SEVENTH WEEK OF THE YEAR
Jon 3:1-10 and Lk 10:38-42

There is a famous line from Isaiah which goes, "Here I am, Lord, send me." It is a spontaneous statement in which Isaiah volunteers himself to serve in the ministry. When Jonah was asked to go on a ministerial mission, there was a spirit within him which said something like, "Here I am, Lord, but don't send me." It was that rebellious spirit which lay behind the dire difficulties of this prophet. He had been directed to Nineveh, but since he hated this capital city of the dreaded Assyrians, he went in the opposite direction. Israel had been captive too long and suffered too many humiliations, at the hands of the Assyrians for Jonah now to be friendly to them. He hated them so much, he didn't even want them to hear God's word. His decision and attempt to flee from Nineveh and sail to Tarshish instead is a classic example of running from God, instead of running with God. After a type of messianic death and resurrection in which he entered the fish's belly and was spewed out again in three days, he became a new spiritual man. A second chance was offered him to preach in Nineveh and this time he says, "Gladly!" He had seen enough of the inside of a fish's belly. God's trademark is the second chance. If we have not been following our calling, today he offers us another chance.

WEDNESDAY, TWENTY-SEVENTH WEEK OF THE YEAR
Jon 4:1-11 and Lk 11:1-4

Today we conclude the Book of Jonah with the liturgical reading of the fourth and last chapter. The story shows Jonah still being influenced by his old ideas of intolerance, but God continues to instruct him patiently to the end. We might wonder why Jonah can't simply give up his own way of thinking and accept the instructions of the Lord. Before we are too hard on him, we should ask, "Why can't we?" Do we in some ways try to flee from God, rather than face reality and be converted to the truth? Can we think of some personal death-resurrection experiences, when we promised to begin a new life but failed to follow through? These could be times of personal sickness, an operation, a serious financial loss, death in the immediate family, etc. Often the more remote these become, the more we return to being our old selves again. We, like Jonah, are called to be more tolerant in our views of other people — even our enemies. Do we really believe God loves all people, regardless of their religious denominations, nationality or past evil deeds? Have we grown at least a bit, by our re-reading and praying over the Book of Jonah?

THURSDAY, TWENTY-SEVENTH WEEK OF THE YEAR
Ml 3:13-20 and Lk 11:5-13

To get the full impact of a Scripture passage we must view it in its context. In this Gospel passage, Jesus is replying to the apostles' question about how to pray. The Lord answers their inquiry with the story of the "Midnight Visitor." Imagine someone ringing your doorbell or pounding on your door at midnight. You, no doubt, would be very reluctant to get up to let him in, possibly because of sleepiness, but especially because of fear. If the ringing and knocking continued, you would have to deal with the situation in some way. If the doorbell rang only once and then the person left, there would be no problem. The door simply would not be answered. It is the persistence that makes the difference. Jesus says that it is persistence in prayer that causes prayers to be answered. Jesus is the friend within. It is the Lord who works the night shift. We can ask, seek, or knock anytime of the day or night. A recent survey revealed that 56% of the Catholics in the U.S.A. consider praying to be the most important part of their faith. A prayer offered without perseverance, though, is hardly a prayer. Remember the "Midnight Visitor" and what really caused the door to be answered.

FRIDAY, TWENTY-SEVENTH WEEK OF THE YEAR
Jl 1:13-15; 2:1-2 and Lk 11:15-26

A TV preacher recently bellowed how Jesus was about to "put the devil into bondage." "Satan will be knocked down; so look out, devil!" he shouted. The people applauded and cheered. Many are attracted to this kind of theatrical dramatics, for that seems to clarify, in a very simple way, the complex and oftentimes confusing problem of evil. The implication is that it's the devil who is the cause of all the evil and sin in the world. That means, therefore, that I am not personally the cause of my sin. I'm a good person. If the devil would let me alone, I would be a saint. The truth, though, is that if the devil would die today — be completely annihilated — evil would still exist, for it lives and thrives within human nature. St. Paul spoke of fighting evil within his own nature. He said that he knew what he should do and avoid, but many times he did just the opposite. We are to see Jesus, not primarily as a "devil downer," but as a "people uplifter." Our lives are not lived under the influence of the devil so much as they are lived under the influence of our own free, often sinful, choices. God's strength and grace exist for our benefit. Jesus died and rose, not to destroy the devil by his power, but to save us by his blood.

SATURDAY, TWENTY-SEVENTH WEEK OF THE YEAR
Jl 4:12-21 and Lk 11:27-28

This Gospel passage from Luke is the shortest Gospel in our eucharistic liturgy. It contains only two sentences. Although brief, it says plenty. It's one of my favorites. This is its message to me. Jesus was speaking some very beautiful and profound thoughts to the crowd when a lady with a sincere, motherly heart imagined how proud Mary must have felt because of her wonderful son, Jesus. Being so deeply moved, she loudly voiced her inspired feelings to everyone. Mary was blest, she said, because she had given birth to this outstanding young man. Jesus, in turn, replied to the lady's public comment by saying that his mother was indeed blessed, but that this was so, not because she had given birth to him, but because she had heard God's word and kept it. The fact that she was the mother of the Lord indeed added to her blessedness, but she was blessed long before she became his mother. She is a holy person in her own right, aside from being the mother of Jesus. Only one person can be the mother of the Lord, but millions can be blessed. It's not my title nor position that makes me what I am; it's the virtue and honesty in my heart.

MONDAY, TWENTY-EIGHTH WEEK OF THE YEAR
Rm 1:1-7 and Lk 11:29-32

Today we begin reading from Paul's Letter to the Romans. It's a long letter and will continue in our daily liturgy for a month. This letter is a bit different from most of his others, for they were written after he had preached to those particular people. Romans was written and sent before he went to Rome. It was to introduce himself to the people. Here Paul calls himself "a servant of Jesus Christ." He says he's glad to preach a Gospel which was promised long ago by the Hebrew prophets. His purpose is to explain to the people how they can know and love the Son of God. He tells his audience how, in the flesh, Jesus came from the line of King David but how, in the spirit, Jesus is truly God. The people in Rome are called to live in the peace and holiness of Jesus. During the next weeks we will share these thoughts from Paul, just as the Romans did. The letter was written and sent around the year

58. Paul didn't arrive in Rome until three years later, for he was imprisoned in Jerusalem for two years. He worked for about six years in Rome and was martyred there in the year 67. His presence in Rome is still felt today, especially in the magnificent basilica of St. Paul Outside the Walls — built in his honor and memory.

TUESDAY, TWENTY-EIGHTH WEEK OF THE YEAR
Rm 1:16-25 and Lk 11:37-41

The Gospel normally pictures Jesus as a mild, forgiving type of person. False charges were often brought against him and still he remained silent — making no attempt to defend himself. That, however, was not always his style. The Lord could be blunt in his approach and his words could as easily offend as they could inspire. Take today's Gospel for example. A Pharisee invited the Lord to dinner in his home. Jesus omitted the customary ceremonial washing of the cups and dishes before eating. The outside of the cups and dishes were religiously washed before meals, even though they were already clean. Jesus considered it a meaningless and empty ritual. So he didn't do it. The Pharisee called it to his attention and Jesus responded with a bit of fire in his voice. He said it's not the outside that needs to be clean, but the inside. And the same thing applies to people. Although sitting at the Pharisee's table, he called them all "fools." You wonder if the meal was a pleasant experience. We are gathered for a meal. We don't want to be fools, so we must be more than externally clean. Truly spiritual people concentrate on the interior life.

WEDNESDAY, TWENTY-EIGHTH WEEK OF THE YEAR
Rm 2:1-11 and Lk 11:42-46

Paul states in this passage we are all guilty of sin. If we could clearly see the sins that others have committed and the temptations they have endured, we would probably find them similar to our own. However, most of our sins are mercifully kept hidden from other people. Sometimes we become aware of others' sins and we are quick to condemn them. Even when we have no real evidence that others have sinned, our suspicious minds often accuse them. Paul tells us that this is inexcusable. In doing this we convict ourselves, for we are guilty of similar misdeeds. But since our sins are often secret, we deceptively act as though we are very righteous. There is a question posed in this passage, in verse 4, which reveals a terrific and extraordinary insight into the mercy of God. The question is: "Do you not know that God's kindness is an invitation to you to repent?" Quietly and patiently, God waits for us to run the course of our selfish and sinful ways. His mercy holds punishment in check, wanting only to extend forgiveness when we are ready to reform. The Lord knows my weak human nature and is therefore tolerant with me. If God were to strike out with justified punishment after a few failures, I would not have a chance. In the same way, I must be patient with the sinful weaknesses of others.

THURSDAY, TWENTY-EIGHTH WEEK OF THE YEAR
Rm 3:21-29 and Lk 11:47-54

Telling the truth can be dangerous to the speaker, for truth can make people uncomfortable and cause them to lash out in a revengeful manner. Well aware of that, Jesus is nonetheless blunt and right to the point as he speaks his mind in today's Gospel story. The Lord is like the prophets of old who likewise simply spoke the truth, which often provoked others to the point of killing them. Abel was most generous to God, while Cain was selfish. Cain did not want to be constantly reminded of his short-comings, so he killed his brother rather than reform himself. It was the first of a long series of killing sacred messengers. The phrase Jesus uses about erecting the tombs of the prophets meant that those who honored the prophets after their death bore at least some responsibility for sending them to their death in the first place. The truth refuses to die for, ironically, prophets often become even more popular and powerful after being killed for a cause in which they believed. Such was the case of Jesus. His life inspires us; his death saves us. He, like so many with a noble message, are heard only after they die. To die for a cause in which you believe is the ultimate sign of true conviction. Spilled blood speaks even more convincingly than courageous voices.

FRIDAY, TWENTY-EIGHTH WEEK OF THE YEAR
Rm 4:1-8 and Lk 12:1-7

A lot of people enjoy spending time and energy in the pursuit of their family genealogies. We like to know about our ancestors and speak of them with pride. If there is someone in our family history who was famous and popular, we are all the more eager to let people know about it. The more we know our ancestors, the better we know ourselves, for from them we have inherited a lot of our characteristics. Paul calls Abraham his ancestor in the flesh, and speaks proudly of him. We, too, call Abraham our father in faith and feel the same pride. When we read of the wonderful accomplishments of our ancestors in faith, we ought to beam with pride. We should want to learn all we can about them and try to imitate them. If we consider them as the spiritual ancestors they truly are, then we can more easily think of one another as brothers and sisters, regardless of color, nationality or personal beliefs. Our goal, as Christians, is to develop such a love and caring concern for each other that we truly consider ourselves as part of one universal family. By thinking and acting in such a way we are accomplishing at least one of the objectives for which Jesus came into the world and gave his life.

SATURDAY, TWENTY-EIGHTH WEEK OF THE YEAR
Rm 4:13, 16-18 and Lk 12:8-12

There's a very strong statement in this Gospel passage: ". . . whoever blasphemes the Holy Spirit will never be forgiven." The term blasphemy is a Greek word meaning to use abusive language toward God or sacred things. The Old Testament has many examples where blasphemy is condemned. In Leviticus (24:16) we find that blasphemy is punishable by death. In the New Testament Jesus is accused of being guilty of blasphemy when he forgives sin and when he claims to be the Messiah. The stern warning to avoid blasphemy against the Holy Spirit, which Jesus utters in today's Gospel, follows shortly after he is accused of casting out devils by the power of the devil. Such a sin will not be forgiven — not because God cannot forgive it — but because the person guilty of the blasphemy is unable to request God's forgiveness. How can one ask to receive forgiveness from God, if the person does not believe that God can forgive? Jesus says that people may speak against him as the "Son of Man" and they will be forgiven, for someone may truly not understand his divine and human nature. That is excusable. But if a person is made aware of the true nature of Jesus, then the Lord is to be accepted. The person who blasphemes against the Holy Spirit knows the truth and not only refuses to accept it, but calls truth falsehood. God is equated with the evil one. May the Holy Spirit of Truth lead us all to the eternal truth.

MONDAY, TWENTY-NINTH WEEK OF THE YEAR
Rm 4:20-25 and Lk 12:13-21

Paul reminisces to the Romans, in this reading, about his ancestor Abraham. He says Abraham had a basic religious creed to guide his life and the same can direct us. His governing principle was: "If God promised it, God will do it." Where did Abraham acquire the lofty promises of God? He must have discovered them in his heart, anchored there from his many conversations with his creator in prayer. God, no doubt, spoke to Abraham through inspirations, the same way God speaks to us. Abraham's faith did not come from books, the synagogue, the church or classrooms. He was a primitive person, but very much in tune with the spiritual world. It's amazing to think of the depth of his faith, for he lived before the Ten Commandments were given and prior to the Prophets. He had no Bible. He lived far off and long ago but, for us, he remains an excellent spiritual guide. His name means "Father of many nations." That includes the U.S.A. where Lincoln, our most outstanding president, was also called Abraham. Do we have the sustaining faith of Abraham in our hearts? Our faith really ought to surpass his, for we have so many more blessings, especially those that have come through the death and resurrection of Jesus.

TUESDAY, TWENTY-NINTH WEEK OF THE YEAR
Rm 5:12-15, 17-19, 20-21 and Lk 12:35-38

If we have a 7:00 p.m. appointment with someone, we arrange our schedule to be available at the time. We know the person may be five minutes early or late and we must adjust to it. Even with our schedules and appointments, events and happenings don't flow flawlessly. There is always present the knowledge that we must expect the unexpected. Vivid pictures are still in our minds of the baseball fans gathering in San Francisco to watch the World Series only to have the game, and their lives, interrupted and disrupted by that devastating earthquake. The timing was ironic and totally unexpected. Jesus tells us to be alert to God's presence in our lives in just the same fashion. The servant must be ready to open the door for the master who comes home late from a wedding reception. God comes to us at unexpected times and in unexpected places. It may be at midnight or sunrise; we may be in bed or out on the road. We especially try to hear the voice of God while in church, during the reading of Scripture, the preaching of the homily, the singing of the hymns, the reception of holy communion or in the quiet times when we pause for the purpose of prayer. Expect to receive an inspiration today. It may come when you least expect it. We wonder what the message will be. Be ready now to hear and to accept it.

WEDNESDAY, TWENTY-NINTH WEEK OF THE YEAR
Rm 6:12-18 and Lk 12:39-48

Five different times the terms "slaves and slavery" are mentioned in the first reading, and the same theme continues in the Gospel. A slave, literally, is a human being who is owned by another human. Although it is a most degrading situation, some have seen the beginning of slavery as a step toward civilization. Their reasoning goes something like this. In very primitive times the prisoners of war were killed. That was barbaric. Then the prisoners were spared and became slaves to the conquerors. They were given no pay, but were provided with food, clothing and shelter. That was a step up from being killed. A further development was to become a serf. They worked the land and could personally keep some of the produce, although they paid a high tax to their owners. The ultimate step was to become a free man or woman. The African slave trade in the 16th century, practiced by Spain and Portugal, was a totally different matter. In this more ancient concept of slavery, Paul sees the Christian as a slave of God, who is the Good Master. God provides a household, food and clothing. We serve God. We don't want to be freed or separated from the Master. Being a slave of God is not re-pugnant. We will receive no abuse from such a Master — only blessings. It is another way of saying that we are dedicated entirely to the Lord.

THURSDAY, TWENTY-NINTH WEEK OF THE YEAR
Rm 6:19-23 and Lk 12:49-53

It would be a mistake to think that Jesus preached a message of peace at all costs. True, the Lord was a peacemaker but he was also a "troublemaker and rebel." The quote here is very explicit: "Do you think I have come to establish peace on earth? I assure you the contrary is true." Christianity divides people today as well as unites them. We are divided over such religious and moral questions as birth control, abortion, marriage outside the Church, capital punishment, war, passivism, just taxes, etc. Among various Christian denominations there are serious differences of opinions about the virgin birth of Jesus, degree of honor for Mary, interfaith communion, proper Church authority, etc. Different ways of viewing the same religious questions have been operative in the Church since the first centuries. The Antioch School in Syria gave a literal interpretation to Scripture on various religious questions, while the Alexandrian School in Egypt favored a figurative one. We expect divisions but respect each other's views. Jesus does not actively promote division, but he does solicit our sincere commitment to him and, when we give it, divisions often result.

FRIDAY, TWENTY-NINTH WEEK OF THE YEAR
Rm 7:18-25 and Lk 12:54-59

Commentators say that Paul is not so much speaking here in an autobiographical manner as he is reflecting on the inner struggle which is common to us all. The Jewish law, in which he was well schooled, taught that there are two instinctive impulses within each person. One leads to good and the other to evil. Each is constantly vying for supremacy. The good impulses come from God and the evil ones from ourselves or, as Paul says, "from the flesh." Experience shows that it is the flesh which holds a commanding lead in victories over the spirit. Introspection reveals that this same battle rages within each one of us. We all have the proverbial "Achilles' heel." Weaknesses of the flesh come in many forms: anger, pride, sloth, dishonesty, unbridled ambition, greed, irresponsibility, uncontrolled sexual desires, excessive dependence on alcohol, food, etc. When we think of our many weaknesses, we are inclined to cry out with Paul: "What a wretched man (or woman) I am!" The one who can free us from these evil powers of fleshly domination is the same for us as it was for Paul: our risen Savior. And so, with Paul, we proclaim as we chant our victory hymn of praise, "All glory, honor and praise to God, through Jesus Christ our Lord!"

SATURDAY, TWENTY-NINTH WEEK OF THE YEAR
Rm 8:1-11 and Lk 13:1-9

In this Gospel, Jesus mentions two incidents which actually took place in Palestine at the time. The fact that he mentions them shows him as a true historical person, very much aware of current events in and around Jerusalem. One of these incidents is an act of violence perpetrated by Pilate who ordered some Galilean Jews killed while they were offering their religious sacrifices. The same Pilate would soon condemn Jesus himself to death. The other incident involved a construction accident in Siloam. In both cases, a number of people lost their lives. Jesus takes the occasion to emphasize that these deaths did not occur because the people involved were guilty of sin, or were being punished by

God. He tells us clearly that they were not any more guilty, or deserving to die, than any one else. It was common then, as it is now, to associate disaster with some type of punishment. We often wonder why certain people, seemingly innocent, suffer untimely accidents and deaths. In their confusion, some say, "God is trying to tell us something." When we are faced with perplexing questions about such tragedies, let us think of this passage and respond that God is, indeed, trying to tell us something — that such events do not stem from personal guilt. They are mysteries. They can also be occasions of grace for those who reflect on the uncertainties of life.

MONDAY, THIRTIETH WEEK OF THE YEAR
Rm 8:12-17 and Lk 13:10-17

The Jewish Sabbath required the people to worship and rest. Often they objected to the way Jesus observed it — not about his lack of worship, but his refusal to rest. It seems that there was more emphasis on resting than on worshipping. In fact, the word "Sabbath" is from the Hebrew meaning "to rest," and through the centuries the Jewish people had adhered to a very orthodox interpretation. After the Babylonian Exile in 587 B.C., the Sabbath observance became very strict. The law listed 39 different kinds of labor which were forbidden on the Sabbath. These included such things as bearing burdens, gathering sticks, lighting fires and travelling more than a Sabbath's day journey — less than a mile. In his attempt to update the old laws, and especially to help people, Jesus irritated those who favored the traditional observance. Whether we are worshipping, resting or doing good deeds, we are fulfilling our "Sabbath observance" in a very exemplary manner. Jesus said we were not made for the Sabbath, but that the Sabbath was made for us.

TUESDAY, THIRTIETH WEEK OF THE YEAR
Rm 8:18-25 and Lk 13:18-21

If we gave medals of honor to biblical personalities, St. Paul no doubt would win the "most energetic award." He never seemed to tire in his very ambitious schedule of preaching, travelling, writing and even suffering for Jesus. Paul is an inspiration for all times, but especially for these days when so many seem to give up or burn out. It seems that we often get to a point where we just don't care any longer and our energy level falls to zero. What was his secret? What motivated and enabled him to continue and be successful, often in spite of terrific odds? The answer is contained in the first sentence of this reading from the famous eighth chapter of his letter to the Romans. "I consider the sufferings of the present to be as nothing compared with the glory to be revealed in us" (Rm 8:18). Because he possessed such deep and enduring hope, he could find strength for every task and carry on his work with "patient endurance." We try to accomplish many worthwhile deeds in our lives, striving to help others and to make the world a better place in which to live. When discouragement begins to sap our energies, hope for a better future can renew our strength, enable us to cope with adverse circumstances, and help us to carry on with patient endurance.

WEDNESDAY, THIRTIETH WEEK OF THE YEAR
Rm 8:26-30 and Lk 13:22-30

Any sheepherder, farmer, or agricultural person in general at the time of Jesus would have known what the Lord meant by the "narrow door." The narrow door is still seen in our barns today and it serves the same purpose. It's a small door on hinges, which is cut into the large barn door, which is heavy and rolls on a track. The large door is necessary for the passage of the big equipment in and out of the barn. It's also used when there is a herd of cattle or flock of sheep. Operating the large door requires considerable effort because it must be kept well secured in case of a severe wind storm. Because of its weight, it is often difficult to push open. The narrow door, usually cut into the larger one, swings open easily for a person to enter. Only one person at a time is able to enter the narrow door. Jesus seems to imply in his response that people won't be entering the kingdom in gigantic throngs, which is, indeed, a sobering thought. Someone was once asked why he wanted to go to heaven. He replied, with this Scripture text in mind, "For all the usual reasons plus one — I don't like crowds."

THURSDAY, THIRTIETH WEEK OF THE YEAR
Rm 8:31-39 and Lk 13:31-35

Today's reading is another powerful passage from Romans which concludes this illustrious chapter eight. The first line contains so much meaning that it has been set to music: "If God is with us, who can be against us?" Paul tells us here that there is no limit to God's love for us and no limit to what God will do for us. This limitless love of God is staggering. The Apostle put it this way, "Is it possible that he who did not spare his own Son but handed him over for the sake of us all will not grant us all things besides?" Can any gift be greater than the gift of God's own Son? Furthermore, the Son was given not only to live among us, but to die for us. From God, therefore, we truly can expect the unexpected. As human beings, we find it hard to appreciate this depth of love, for we don't operate on that level. We are not that generous with our gifts. Paul concludes that, because we have received the most exalted gift imaginable — life in Jesus, there can be no distress or persecution which could ever separate us from God's love. Can we agree with Paul that nothing will ever separate us from the love of God that comes to us in Christ Jesus? Not the height of glory or the depth of despair, no creature not even an angel, not even death?

FRIDAY, THIRTIETH WEEK OF THE YEAR
Rm 9:1-5 and Lk 14:1-6

Luke, the doctor, uses the technical medical term "dropsy" to diagnose the disease of the man who was cured by Jesus. Dropsy is a build-up of excess water in the cavities of the body. We're told that this cure was performed on the occasion of Jesus' coming to eat a meal at the home of a leading Pharisee. Considering all the opposition that Jesus gave the Pharisees, you wonder why they continued to invite him to dinner. The circumstances here make one think it might have been a set-up, to find some way to accuse the Lord. Why was the suffering man seated directly in front of Jesus? It was the Sabbath day and other Pharisees and lawyers were present. When cured, why did the man leave and not stay for dinner? Was he there not to dine but to put Jesus to the test for the Pharisees? Isn't it good to know that Jesus feels compelled to heal people even before the meal on the Sabbath? The same divine physician heals us before our eucharistic meals, rescuing us from the pit, Sabbath or not. Today we may be filled with hatred, jealousy, pride or "spiritual dropsy." Mercy is ours for the asking.

SATURDAY, THIRTIETH WEEK OF THE YEAR
Rm 11:1-2, 11-12, 25-29 and Lk 14:1, 7-11

Jesus explains the code of conduct to be observed when invited to a wedding reception. Those seated nearest the head table will get their food sooner than those in the back. Some people, in their selfish excitement to get the front tables, may sit where there is a "reserved" sign. Perhaps they won't notice the sign, or maybe they'll ignore it; until, that is, some family member of the bride and groom arrive for whom the table has been saved. Then those who had pushed their way to the front will be relegated to the section near the door, for the other tables at this point will now be taken. The eucharistic meal is often spoken of in terms of a wedding feast. We are invited. Some pious persons, very respectfully, don't take the front seats nor even the last ones — they stand along the back wall. A few even stay in the vestibule. The Lord's words, "My friend, come up higher," now applies to them. We are celebrating our faith, and you are part of the family of faith. You belong. A personal invitation was prepared by the Lord's death and extended to us in baptism. We are friends and family. We're always invited to come up higher.

MONDAY, THIRTY-FIRST WEEK OF THE YEAR
Rm 11:29-36 and Lk 14:12-14

We profess that God knows all there is to know. Imagine a mind so brilliant that there are no unanswered questions, no mysteries or doubts, perfect knowledge on every subject. What fantastic type of intellectual life that would be! This is the calibre of God's knowledge, and it extends to the ancient past and goes forward into the never-ending future. Perfect knowledge rules out the concept of time, for God lives a kind of timeless existence. All things, for him, are happening, as it were, simultaneously. Some philosophers and theologians tell us that God dwells beyond time in eternity, where there is no succession of moments but all is one big present reality. Paul is so impressed as he expounds on the wisdom and knowledge of God that he calls God's ways "unsearchable." When we find life confusing, our questions unanswered, or things happening in a way we can't understand or accept, we might think that God is to blame and that we are being ignored or punished. How much better it would be to realize that our small minds cannot begin to fathom the mysteries of life. The best response we can make is to be found in those time-honored words: "Thy will be done."

TUESDAY, THIRTY-FIRST WEEK OF THE YEAR
Rm 12:5-16 and Lk 14:15-24

Jesus was at a party and the table conversation inspired him to tell those sitting nearby a "party parable" about the kingdom. The key point of this story is that the Lord gives a dinner in the kingdom, and we're all invited. Some flippantly ignore the invitation because they have stronger attachments to real estate, livestock, and marital matters. The Lord and Master had placed much time and effort into this meal and did not take the rejections lightly. His altruism turned to anger and he quickly invited other extremely hungry and less fortunate people who would truly appreciate the invitation. We can not truly appreciate the sacred party of the eucharistic liturgy if we're overly preoccupied with our thoughts of real estate, livestock and social commitments. The story says the first invited guests did not have a good reason for refusing. If their reasons would have been more valid, the host would have been less irritated. Our salvation, like the party itself, is a free gift. It was prepared for each of us at a very great cost. We should accept our personal invitation to the banquet. No other worldly affair should be preferred, or keep us from being present.

WEDNESDAY, THIRTY-FIRST WEEK OF THE YEAR
Rm 13:8-10 and Lk 14:25-33

On this particular occasion, Luke says there was a great crowd with Jesus. But the Lord makes the point in the parable that, though they were in his presence, they were not all really with him. To be with him, Jesus said, two things are necessary. The first is: Don't be excessively attached to other people, or to worldly possessions. It's amazing how much we must often sacrifice in order to achieve something really valuable. Kenny Rogers sings about knowing "when to hold 'em and when to fold 'em." Jesus says you must be willing to "turn your back" on others, your family and even your own desires, in order to be a true disciple of God. The second requirement necessary to be with Jesus is: Being willing to suffer for him. We all carry a cross of some kind; it's part of our life situation. Regardless of how large or heavy anyone's cross may seem, it will always be only minuscule and bantam weight in comparison to the cross that Jesus bore. We, who are disciples, with our mini-crosses, are all to follow the one carrying the gigantic cross. Just being baptized, or attending church or receiving communion, doesn't make us "with the Lord." Being here, dispossessed and prepared to suffer for God, makes us truly "with him," and in possession of his friendship.

THURSDAY, THIRTY-FIRST WEEK OF THE YEAR
Rm 14:7-12 and Lk 15:1-10

They insidiously whispered against Jesus, "This man associates with sinners and eats with them." We can just imagine the juicy gossip. If you or I were attacked thus, we might reply in anger, "I do not." Jesus, however, affirmed the charge and openly admitted that he did associate with sinners and eat with them. Isn't it wonderful that he said that? Now we can approach the Lord in prayer, worship and communion with confidence. We would be very frightened to come to the altar if we thought Jesus didn't want to have anything to do with sinners. On our part we should not try to justify ourselves by saying we are not sinners, but should rather admit that we are and be very thankful that Jesus welcomes us. We do our conscience violence and disturb our peace of mind when we try to make believe we don't sin. We do sin. Everyone does. But that doesn't mean we are alienated from God. In fact, strange as it might seem, our sinfulness draws us into a closer relationship with God, for we realize how much we depend on God's mercy and forgiveness. The one who says he has no sin, John says, is a liar. When I am weak, then I am strong.

FRIDAY, THIRTY-FIRST WEEK OF THE YEAR
Rm 15:14-21 and Lk 16:1-8

We are naturally concerned about the future, as is the man in this Gospel story. His worry about sufficient money for his old age may have led him to be dishonest in the first place. Now, without a job, he really had reason to worry. There is no doubt that this man was street-wise and he applied his cunning to provide for his future. He had to work fast, for there was very little time to make his deals. Once he was dismissed from office, he would have no opportunity to forego his commission on the money owed his master in order to gain favors from his master's debtors. So he alters the books and transacts "deals" with them in order to acquire some future security. This is a typical parable, making just one strong point. The point is: we are to be as enterprising in securing our future in heaven as he was in providing for his future here on earth. We admire his concern to prepare for the future, but we don't approve of the means he used. Jesus highlights the key point of the parable and tells us that we are to use all the ingenuity we have to achieve lasting security. Like the man in the parable, we can't do it alone. That's where our faith can assist us. We should "make a deal" with the Lord.

SATURDAY, THIRTY-FIRST WEEK OF THE YEAR
Rm 16:3-9, 16, 22-27 and Lk 16:9-15

After many daily readings, we now have reached the conclusion of the letter to the Romans. We have seen, interwoven among its sixteen chapters and many verses, Paul's keen sense of biblical history and his knowledge of contemporary Christians. The letter speaks eloquently about the deep and hidden mysteries of God. We now are the contemporary Christians, like our first century counterparts. The letter can serve us as surely as it did them. Each time we read a book of the Bible or even one passage of Scripture, we can gain new insights into its meaning. The meanings are often colored by the particular mood we are in during our reading. When sad, one passage may affect us very differently than it would were we in a happy frame of mind. Scripture is meant to bring God's light to us, as it did to the Romans. Return again to this letter and reread what Paul has to say about faith in Jesus, the meaning of justification, and the duties of the Christian life. The thoughts he expresses in chapter twelve should be remembered and lived: "Your love must be sincere. Detest what is evil, cling to what is good. . . . Rejoice in hope, be patient under trial, persevere in prayer."

MONDAY, THIRTY-SECOND WEEK OF THE YEAR
Ws 1:1-7 and Lk 17:1-6

Here's the right thing to do when someone does you wrong. Forgive that person from your heart. If and when the offender says, "I'm sorry," grant him or her pardon right away. Our forgiveness must be of a certain quality; it must be unconditional — no limiting circumstances, just flat-out forgiveness. Luke says that we are to extend pardon, as a minimum, seven times a day, seven days a week. Why not try to forgive at least the minimum number of times today? Even if the one who has offended you says nothing, you can still let this "clemency principle" operate within you. My guess is that you could probably reach your quota of seven simply driving to work. The words of Jesus, as recorded in Matthew 18:22, are even more ambitious. There the "maximum" number of pardons expected exceeds 490 (more than 70x7). Wouldn't it be challenging to offer that many pardons someday? You'd need a small pocket counter just to keep track. You could call it "vindication day," and set out to be at peace with everyone. We could easily imagine 490 opportunities to practice patience and forgiveness in our associations with one another at work, at school, with the members of our families, on the phone, in traffic, and so forth. Kind treatment of others is the best assurance that we will be treated kindly in return. Can we be more generous in our forgiveness today?

TUESDAY, THIRTY-SECOND WEEK OF THE YEAR
Ws 2:23 - 3:9 and Lk 17:7-10

What does it mean to be made in the image and likeness of God? The phrase first appears in Genesis and here, in the Book of Wisdom, it is repeated. The meaning may be that human beings, like God, have intelligence and decision making powers. One author says it means we rule the rest of creation like God, since we stand upright and therefore are elevated above the other animals. Self-consciousness and self-determination may also be part of what it means to be made in the image and likeness of God. Here in the Book of Wisdom yet another aspect is presented. The author says that God made us "to be imperishable; the image of his own nature. . . ." Today we refer to this concept when we speak of immortality. The Genesis story implies that our physical imperishableness was intended but then lost through sin, but that our spiritual imperishableness continues. There are literally hundreds of qualities that come to mind when we think of the image of God. So when the Bible tells us that we are made in that same image, it is affirming the tremendous dignity which is conferred upon all who are born with a human nature. No wonder this passage is a favorite to be read at the time of a funeral.

WEDNESDAY, THIRTY-SECOND WEEK OF THE YEAR
Ws 6:2-11 and Lk 17:11-19

Today's reading is addressed to those "who are in power over the multitudes." Leaders, who take their responsibilities seriously, have a tremendous burden placed on them. They must walk the fine line between giving direction and yet not lording it over people. They are to promote the public good and yet not violate the rights of individuals. When young Solomon was approaching the office of king of Israel, he asked for the gift of wisdom to rule the people fairly. Present-day leaders should think more in terms of asking advice, rather than giving orders without adequate consultation from others. This applies to both civil and Church leaders. This Scripture passage exhorts leaders to have a vital, inner determination to be firm and fair to all. This implies not just the possession of intellectual knowledge but a unique type of leadership skill as well. As the Lord scrutinizes the counsels of our modern-day leaders, we wonder who among them is uniquely divinely approved as doing an exemplary job. Since the law teaches as well as polices, those who make the laws need more qualifications than just getting voted into office. They need inner wisdom. The "leadership look" is to be found not in the face or in the clothes but in the heart.

THURSDAY, THIRTY-SECOND WEEK OF THE YEAR
Ws 7:22 - 8:1 and Lk 17:20-25

Today's passage opens with a very long sentence which applauds the venerable quality of wisdom. Wisdom is called "intelligent, holy, unique, certain, kindly, all-powerful, all-seeing," and so forth. Fitting enough for the book that bears its name. Wisdom certainly is unique. It stands above the ordinary kind of knowledge. A person can be very knowledgeable but still not have wisdom, for knowledge can be used for good or evil; wisdom will always be used for good. The poet Alexander Pope wrote: "A little knowledge is a dangerous thing." But that would never be said of wisdom. A little knowledge may make us think we are more intelligent than we really are. Wisdom, however, will remind the truly intelligent how very little they actually understand. Wisdom is God-inspired and always directed toward that which is benevolent. A tiny bit of wisdom is never dangerous; an abundance will not make us conceited. For wisdom, we can confidently work and pray. It will always direct us to the truth.

FRIDAY, THIRTY-SECOND WEEK OF THE YEAR
Ws 13:1-9 and Lk 17:26-37

We study a work of art to know the artist. The number of creative works produced by millions of people tell us something of the workers who made them. The brilliant St. Thomas Aquinas used this principle to explain one of his most impressive reasons for the existence of God. It's known as the "Order of the Universe" theory and it finds inspiration in this passage from the Book of Wisdom. When you see an elegantly designed watch, consistently displaying the correct time, you know that somewhere there is a very intelligent watchmaker. An impressive painting of the human face or of a multi-colored autumn scene tells you that somewhere there is a very talented artist. When we observe the stupendous clockwork of the planetary system, we should be moved to look beyond to see the responsible maker. The same is true of all that is. All the beauty about us in the rich ambience of nature, and the radiant vitality which shines forth from a million human faces makes us look beyond the creature for the divine artist. Wisdom reminds us (13:5) that "from the greatness and the beauty of created things their original author, by analogy, is seen."

SATURDAY, THIRTY-SECOND WEEK OF THE YEAR
Ws 18:14-16; 19:6-9 and Lk 18:1-8

We don't know the exact time of day that Jesus was born, but there is an ancient tradition of celebrating this wonderful event at midnight. The Christmas Midnight Mass remains very popular in our time. How did it begin? One verse in the Book of Wisdom (18:14) has had a significant influence on the origin of commemorating the birth of Jesus at midnight. The event to which Wisdom refers took place when "the night in its swift course was half spent . . ." This section of Scripture refers to the coming of the avenging angel to Egypt to punish the land for Pharaoh's refusal to release the Hebrew people. The terms "fierce warrior and sharp sword" certainly fit those circumstances better than they do the birth of Jesus. However, Jesus does symbolically fulfill this passage, for he truly is a spiritual warrior combating evil. The Savior, like the avenging angel, bounded from heaven to lead his people out of slavery into a freedom of the spirit. We can happily reflect on the many freedoms which we possess, both in our country and in our Church. Each day (and each midnight) present opportunities for us to invite Jesus to be born again in our lives, to come and set us free.

MONDAY, THIRTY-THIRD WEEK OF THE YEAR
1 M 1:10-15, 41-43, 54-57, 62-63 and Lk 18:35-43

Visiting Jericho on a warm spring afternoon is a delightful experience. The air is flower and blossom scented, the freshly squeezed orange juice is delicious, and the ancient city is filled with a heavenly ambience. The 5,300 people who live in this present-day West Bank city boast of a proud past. Zacchaeus, the tax collector of sycamore tree-climbing fame, was at one time a citizen there. Another was the blind man whom we meet in this Gospel. Luke leaves him nameless, but Mark calls him Bartimaeus. When Jesus passed through the town, it was Bartimaeus who poured out his heart in that prayer of eight, well-chosen words, which caught the Lord's attention and moved him to compassion: "Jesus, Son of David, have pity on me!" Asked by the Lord why he had prayed so, Bartimaeus replied that he wanted to see. On the spot, his request was granted. We all need to pray that we might see. We need to see goodness in others, see hope in the world, see forgiveness in action. We need to have insight into ourselves. Christ still passes by, through the small towns and back roads of society. We pray to see the will of God in our land, in our neighbors and in ourselves.

TUESDAY, THIRTY-THIRD WEEK OF THE YEAR
2 M 6:18-31 and Lk 19:1-10

Our lives, thoughts and actions are not isolated or totally private matters. What we do and say have effects on others. Who we are helps to shape others in the formation of their lives, whether we realize it or not. In this scriptural passage, the ninety-year-old Eleazar is put to the test of choosing between his religious beliefs and death. When Eleazar says he will die rather than violate his religion and offend God, his persecutors try to reason with him because of his advanced age and their long association with him. They wanted him to publicly eat pork as a sign of denying his faith. His persecutors, wishing to spare his life, even suggested he bring his own kosher meat and pretend it was pork. That's all he had to do in order to live. He refused, not only because of his own conscience, but especially because he did not want to give poor example to the young. Thus he died a martyr's death. The author says his death became "a model of courage and an unforgettable example of virtue." And how true that statement turned out to be, for at this very moment, we are again admiring Eleazar and praising God for his fortitude and his faith. When facing tough choices between what is correct and what is convenient let's always remember Eleazar.

WEDNESDAY, THIRTY-THIRD WEEK OF THE YEAR
2 M 7:1, 20-31 and Lk 19:11-28

In yesterday's reading, ninety-year-old Eleazar accepted death rather than violate his conscience or give poor example to the young. Today the scene switches to the young, and they prove themselves to be as strong as those who are older. The youngest boy of the family, along with his mother, had witnessed the courageous deaths of his six older brothers. He, like Eleazar, is given the opportunity to avoid death if only "he would abandon his ancestral customs." When the persecuting King Antiochus asked his mother to dissuade him, she only encouraged him to persevere and to die rather than to deny his faith. He, like his brothers, chose to accept the martyr's death and so did his mother. Who would fault any mother who might use questionable tactics to keep her children alive? Since her six older sons had all been martyred, she might have reasonably told the youngest to do anything necessary to avoid death. Yet that was not her decision. These stories from the Books of Maccabees give hints of what would happen a century or so later on Calvary. There would be a flogging, a public trial and a general spectacle. A young man would make a choice to die, and his mother would be there to give him courage. It would become a never-to-be-forgotten scene.

THURSDAY, THIRTY-THIRD WEEK OF THE YEAR
1 M 2:15-29 and Lk 19:41-44

We don't read very often of Jesus weeping, but in this passage we are told that he wept over the city of Jerusalem. The Lord was not lamenting the deterioration of its streets, bridges and buildings, but the spiritual desolation of its people. He cries because they have not learned how to live in peace with each other. In many ways, the old city has not changed much today from the way it was in the time of Jesus. That is true, both of the physical make-up of the city and the spiritual make-up of the people. The massive stone wall still surrounds the old city, and an equal hardness of heart continues to isolate the Moslems, Christians and Jews. Jerusalem is the only city in the world to which three major world religions lay hereditary claim. Ironically, this "city of peace" is anything but a peaceful city. Jerusalem is symptomatic of many cities around the world today. The divisions are wide-spread and apparent: between black and white, rich and poor, honest and criminal, religious and secular, etc. We still continue to be isolated in our own particular ghettoes. Someone has remarked that Sunday morning is the most polarized time in the United States of America. If Jesus came to visit our city, church or family, would he still weep because of our lack of harmony and peace?

FRIDAY, THIRTY-THIRD WEEK OF THE YEAR
1 M 4:36-37 and Lk 19:45-48

On different occasions, when the battles in Israel were ended, the people immediately turned their attention to repairing and rededicating the temple and sanctuaries. Here, the Maccabees follow the same procedure. It was a way of reminding the people that the places of worship are to be held in very high esteem. Jesus followed that same tradition, giving unique honor and sacred respect to the house of prayer. In no way did he want it to be cheapened by worldly commerce. This day we may visit a number of buildings in our city — stores, libraries, post offices, banks, etc., but this building, our house of prayer, is different from all the others. It lifts us out of ourselves, and even out of this world. Our houses of prayer are designed to be beautiful. They are often graced with stained glass windows which inspire in us a sense of prayer. They are meant to be looked at, rather than looked through. When we are on the inside, the sunlight causes the windows to brighten and convey their sacred messages. In our houses of prayer, we meet and communicate with our neighbors and, together, we communicate with our God. Here we especially learn to understand and communicate with ourselves. We should thank God that we have a house of prayer, and use it for that purpose.

SATURDAY, THIRTY-THIRD WEEK OF THE YEAR
1 M 6:1-13 and Lk 20:27-40

Ten kings shared the name of Antiochus, which in Greek means "withstander." The one in today's reading is Antiochus IV. It was his father (Antiochus III, also known as Antiochus the Great) after whom the city of Antioch was named. Antiochus IV is given much adverse coverage in this Book of Maccabees, for he was a constant menace to the Israelites. We see him today, defeated, sick, unable to sleep and facing death. This passage proclaims the teaching that you can't live a life of sin and violence, and be at peace when you come to die. Antiochus had attempted to do that. He is described by historians as eccentric, capricious and belligerent. He went on a military campaign to Egypt and on the way home plundered the Jewish Temple and confiscated all its wealth. He also suppressed Jewish worship, destroyed their sacred books, and imposed Hellenistic customs and pagan festivals on the Jewish people. He also defiantly erected an altar in the sacred Jewish temple to the honor of the Greek god, Zeus. This precipitated the Maccabean revolt. Now on his death bed, Antiochus IV remembers his wicked deeds and feels that he is being punished for them. He laments, "I now recall the evil I did in Jerusalem . . ." I am dying in bitter grief. Eventually our evil deeds catch up with us.

MONDAY, THIRTY-FOURTH WEEK OF THE YEAR
Dn 1:1-6, 8-20 and Lk 21:5-11

It is significant that this poor widow woman contributed two copper coins to the collection basket at the worship service. Had she had but one coin, she would probably have felt pressured to give it, for even though she was materially poor, she was spiritually rich and would have wanted to give something. With only one coin, she would have had no other alternative. But since she had two coins, she could have supported the temple with one and still have kept one for her own needs. If we were extremely poor, and in those circumstances, most of us probably would have given one and kept one. She, however, gave both. Jesus saw her placing the two coins in the basket. He was very impressed by her selfless generosity, and publicly praised her. Generosity in deeds such as this tells a lot about the quality of people. How selfless and giving are we to Church and charity? Do we give to assist, or to get some tax break? It's not stated, but can we not imagine that on the way out of the synagogue, Jesus gave her a whole handful of money? Doesn't Scripture assure us that the Lord will not be outdone in generosity?

TUESDAY, THIRTY-FOURTH WEEK OF THE YEAR
Dn 2:31-45 and Lk 21:5-11

There are some people who would read this passage of Scripture, and others like it, and it would cause them to panic. They would insist that the time is at hand and that the end of the world is imminent. The "end of the world" goes by many different names. It's called the eschaton, the second coming, Armageddon and the rapture. Occasionally we hear of people getting a little bit carried away when it comes to the subject of the end of the world. I heard of one church holding "rapture practices." Many of our fundamentalist brothers and sisters make the teaching of the second coming the center piece of all their theology and keep it before the people always — in their rallies and on the TV screen. Catholic teaching, as well as that of many of the mainline Protestant denominations, takes a much more relaxed attitude toward the "end of the world" issues. We are counselled to avoid being caught up in this excitable flurry of dire predictions. We are warned in Scripture that many will preach in Jesus' name that the end is at hand. The Bible says we are not to follow them and to take care not to be misled. Natural phenomena such as hurricanes and earthquakes often cause people to become frightened that the end of the world is imminent. The approaching end of the second millennium, the year 2000, has also excited a lot of "end of the world" talk. When the world will end, we don't know. More personally and more important is when our lives on earth will come to a conclusion. Remember that Jesus promises new heavens and a new earth. That should over-shadow any fear we have of the world's ending.

WEDNESDAY, THIRTY-FOURTH WEEK OF THE YEAR
Dn 5:1-6, 13-14, 16-17, 23-28 and Lk 21:12-19

When we say we've "seen the writing on the wall," we mean something is going to happen which is unavoidable. That saying takes its origin from the passage we just read from Daniel at this Mass. Belshazzar, King of Babylon, gave a banquet for 1000 lords who were his drinking buddies. When they were under the influence of alcohol, someone brought out of storage the golden and silver vessels which Nebuchadnezzar, father of Belshazzar, had captured from the temple in Jerusalem. It was with these sacred vessels that they toasted their pagan gods. Then suddenly, so the story goes, a human hand appeared and wrote something on the plaster. No one could understand it and so they called the young Hebrew, Daniel, to interpret the writing. The three words spelled doom for the king. His kingdom would be lost and divided and he was being judged inferior in the eyes of God. That is the Old Testament moral. The modern moral is: Don't profane that which is sacred. The human body is sacred; so if you're out drinking with your friends and a writing hand appears, the message is you've had too much to drink. You would do well to find some help and get yourself home.

THURSDAY, THIRTY-FOURTH WEEK OF THE YEAR
Dn 6:12-28 and Lk 21:20-28

The Book of Daniel is written to encourage people in hard times. The first part of the book contains six edifying short stories about the young Hebrew, Daniel, and his friends. Yesterday's account of the writing on the wall was the fifth of these stories. The one today — the episode of Daniel in the lion's den — is the sixth. Daniel violates the order of King Darius which forbade the Hebrews to pray. Daniel is observed praying three times a day and is arrested. His punishment consists of being locked in the lion's den. There, Daniel spends the entire night and remains unharmed. He is then released, the edict is dropped and Darius testifies to the power of the God of Daniel. These stories, of a fictitious nature, are told to give courage to exiled Hebrews.

They are similar to many lives of the saints. Although true in basis, various aspects and virtues are exaggerated in order to edify and impress us. The thinking goes somewhat like this: If these people are so holy and courageous because they believe in God, I also want to believe. Their lives become role models for others, especially the young.

FRIDAY, THIRTY-FOURTH WEEK OF THE YEAR
Dn 7:2-14 and Lk 21:29-33

Again we have a brief, power-packed passage from Luke which presents a striking lesson. "No tree in Palestine appears to be so dead during the winter as the fig tree." So says the well-known Scripture scholar, Carroll Stuhlmueller, C.P. The fig tree is also the one that most vividly announces the springtime, with its profuse blooming. So Jesus called the people to observe the fig tree. This tree is native to the Mediterranean and everyone notices it. In winter, it takes on an emaciated, anemic look. Then, suddenly, with the first sign of spring, it bursts into bloom, and clusters of fruit soon follow. Jesus says that the fig tree is like the word of God. It may seem unattractive, even lifeless. But it is vibrantly alive and can burst into fulfillment suddenly when one least expects it. God's word also will endure. Even if heaven and earth pass away, the word of God will still stand, be alive, bloom and produce fruit. Many of Jesus' commands are very difficult, like loving our enemies and giving away what we possess. When we do these things, we are supposed to find happiness. We must trust that these promises will be fulfilled. God stands behind his word. Picture a seemingly hopeless situation in your life. See what God's word says about it. Realize that its fulfillment may be very close at hand.

SATURDAY, THIRTY-FOURTH WEEK OF THE YEAR
Dn 7:15-27 and Lk 21:34-36

The message from the last reading of this liturgical year is summarized in one word: vigilance. Luke has duly warned his audience of events which will take place, but the implication throughout is that they are not imminent. Even so, the intelligent Christian will not be caught off guard. If we are puffed up with pride, inebriated with alcohol and preoccupied with trivial matters, we will not be prepared for much of anything, certainly not to leave this world. In many ways, the Church emphasizes the call to vigilance. It means to stay awake. We keep our vigil celebrations before major holy days, most notably that of Easter. On that vigil everyone is getting prepared to join in the great day of the Resurrection. On this vigil of a new liturgical year, we might want to join with other people and prepare for the coming year. We could begin our own parish or neighborhood Christian vigilance committee. It would be rewarding to collectively plan for the new Church year which begins with the first Sunday of Advent and to thoughtfully discuss how we can spend it profitably while we wait here on the vigil of eternity.